THE CONCEPT OF THE INDIVIDUAL
IN EIGHTEENTH-CENTURY FRENCH THOUGHT
FROM THE ENLIGHTENMENT
TO THE FRENCH REVOLUTION

THE CONCEPT OF THE INDIVIDUAL
IN EIGHTEENTH-CENTURY FRENCH THOUGHT
FROM THE ENLIGHTENMENT
TO THE FRENCH REVOLUTION

Susan Carpenter Binkley

With a Foreword by
Karlis Racevskis

The Edwin Mellen Press
Lewiston•Queenston•Lampeter

Library of Congress Cataloging-in-Publication Data

Binkley, Susan Carpenter.
  The concept of the individual in eighteenth-century French thought from the
Enlightenment to the French Revolution / Susan Carpenter Binkley ; with a foreword by
Karlis Racevskis.
     p. cm.
  Includes bibliographical references and index.
  ISBN-13: 978-0-7734-5275-6
  ISBN-10: 0-7734-5275-3
  1. Persons. 2. Philosophical anthropology. 3. Philosophy, French--18th century. I.
Title.
  BD450.B4635 2007
  126.0944'09033--dc22

                                                    2007038478

hors série.

A CIP catalog record for this book is available from the British Library.

             The Edwin Mellen Press   The Edwin Mellen Press
                  Box 450   Box 67
             Lewiston, New York   Queenston, Ontario
              USA 14092-0450   CANADA L0S 1L0

                        The Edwin Mellen Press, Ltd.
                        Lampeter, Ceredigion, Wales
                        UNITED KINGDOM SA48 8LT

                    Printed in the United States of America

For my parents

Table of Contents

List of Abbreviations

AP	*Archives parlementaires*
FRF	*Les Femmes dans la Révolution Française*
ORFR	*The Old Regime and the French Revolution*
PW	*Political Writings* (Diderot)
SN	*Système de la nature*
SS	*Système social*
WRP	*Women in Revolutionary Paris 1789-1795*

Foreword

When she was a student, Susan Binkley remembers being puzzled by an apparent paradox. While the French Revolution had obviously brought momentous changes in the political and cultural arenas, the revolutionary period was mainly treated as a void from the perspective of French literary history. The eighteenth century or the Age of Enlightenment, for example, ended on or about 1789 and the nineteenth century began in earnest with the onset of the Romantic movement some three decades later. At the same time, Susan could not help but notice that some momentous changes had taken place during the transitional phase taking French civilization from the eighteenth to the nineteenth century. One such change, she found, was in the concept of the individual, which, in French, was generally indicated by the highly ambivalent – therefore problematic – term *homme* or "man." While those employing the term generally seemed to imply that they used it in a generic, that is not in a gender-specific sense, the word nevertheless seemed to ferry connotations that gave it a weight and repercussions that often belied any claims of neutrality on the part of the users. The desire to clarify this paradox was thus the initial impulse motivating Susan's research project and she began with the assumption that central to the shift that marked the passage from one century to the other was this ambiguous concept of "man."

Pursuing her investigations, Susan discovered that the ambiguity was not limited to the term alone, but appeared to have infected various aspects of revolutionary behavior. Thus she found that the concrete outcomes of revolutionary actions often went counter to the initial, abstract rationales for the actions. The very notion of individual that was used by the revolutionaries to further and justify their cause, proved useful, as well, in denying the freedoms and privileges they had espoused in theory. What makes Susan's arguments especially convincing is her ability to apply the theoretical insights developed by Michel Foucault, whose essays have enabled us to gain a whole new perspective on the Age of Enlightenment. Moreover, the theory of Michel Foucault has been especially pertinent to Susan's project because one of its central concerns has been the evolution and reality of the "subject," that is, the manner in which various social, cultural, and political forces conspire to give form to an individual's identity in Western societies. Thus, in order to dismantle the truths founding our very identity, Foucault found it necessary to go back to the main event founding our modernity – the Enlightenment.

Foucault's critical examination of the Enlightenment, quite understandably, has also served as a motive for placing him in the camp of the postmodernists, since the need to rethink the Enlightenment can be counted among the distinguishing features of what could be considered a typically postmodern critical stance. Indeed, the urge to reexamine the Enlightenment was a characteristic feature of our era, Foucault thought, because a number of socio-political developments marking the second half of the twentieth century had placed the question of the Enlightenment at the heart of several important contemporary concerns. For Foucault, however, the problem of the Enlightenment was not to be posed in terms of a postmodern condition, nor was it a question of the Enlightenment's alleged relevance or irrelevance. Rather than seeking to distinguish the "modern era" from the "premodern" or "postmodern," Foucault suggested, it was more useful to try to find out how the attitude of modernity, ever since its formation, had found itself struggling with attitudes of "countermodernity" (Rabinow 39). In this manner, he thought, we might be able to recapture a critical attitude that he considered to be the most precious part of the Enlightenment's legacy, an attitude he defined as "a philosophical ethos" and as "a permanent critique of our historical era." This critique was to be carried out in terms of an "historical ontology of ourselves," an investigation aimed at answering the question, first suggested by Kant, "what are we in this time which is ours?" The strategy for carrying out this project was to be fundamentally genealogical, since it sought to reveal "in what is given to us as universal, necessary, obligatory, what place is occupied by whatever is singular, contingent, and the product of arbitrary constraints" (Rabinow 45). The ideology of modernity has functioned to validate "universal, necessary, obligatory" definitions purporting to explain who we are in order to forestall any awareness of the contingent and arbitrary nature of the elements forming our identity. The awareness of this subterfuge was, for Foucault, the first step in achieving maturity, even freedom. The obfuscation produced by discourses that imposed universalizing explanations was also dangerous because they served to mask what Foucault saw as a growing threat that the continuous expansion of technical capacities of modern society posed to the freedoms enjoyed by its citizens. It was therefore important to disconnect the "growth of technical capabilities" from "the intensification of power relations" (48). One obvious way in which power relations have gained in intensity is by means of the political uses and misuses of truth. To counteract the politicization of truth effects, Foucault proposed a critical strategy whose aim was to give the subject "the right to question truth concerning its power effects and to question power about its discourses of truth." Consequently, Foucault suggested, "the essential function of critique would be that of desubjectification in the game of what we would call, in a word, the politics of truth" (Schmidt, 386). Such an approach would effectively confront "the question of the relations between the structures of rationality that articulate the true discourse and the mechanisms of subjugation that are tied to it" (391).

What constituted the greatest originality of *The Order of Things* for many of its readers, was the concept of epistemological shifts Foucault had uncovered in the history of Western civilization. Accordingly, what characterizes modern history since the Middle Ages, is its division in three radically discontinuous periods defined by their particular *epistemes*. To appreciate the notion of *episteme*, it is useful to keep in mind the subtitle of *The Order of Things*, which is *An Archaeology of the Human Sciences*. Thus, from the perspective of the metaphor of archaeology, it is possible to view the human sciences as strata of accumulated knowledge – a layering in which each stratum is seen to possess its own particular configuration determined by rules of formation that are the telling characteristics of a given age. Moreover, the layers of civilization are each clearly separated from the others and, "just as the different strata of earth at a dig site tell us little about why one civilization vanished and another began, so the analysis of *epistemes* tells us nothing about the change from one to the other" (Shumway 56).

What is significant about each *episteme* then, is a particular order that accounts for both the possibilities and limits of thinking in a given historical era. It is an ordering process that Foucault identifies as a "middle region," locating it between the empirical manifestations of order or what he calls the "already encoded eye," and a conscious reflection or theorizing aimed at explicating the manifestations of this order. Thus, in every culture, notes Foucault, "between the use of what one might call the ordering codes and reflections upon order itself, there is the pure experience of order and its modes of being" (*The Order of Things* xxi). Works of art as well as of literature assume a privileged role in this regard, because the revelations offered by art or literature can provide indications of an *episteme*'s organizing principles. Art and literature being eminently self-reflexive modes of thought, can be viewed as "meta-epistemic" indicators – that is, as allegorical or symbolic representations of the epistemic patterns that underlie the constitution of knowledge for a given time and place.

It is clearly the kind of understanding that has served as a most useful guide for Susan Binkley's research project and what accounts for the originality of its revelations. The changes in the concept of individuality that Susan discovers and analyzes thus take place because of the conditions created by the revolutionary experience. These were conditions that arose from the need to create a new kind of government and lay the foundations for a new kind of society. In other words, no one had planned or even foreseen these changes: they simply occurred as the attending effects of circumstances that proved to be beyond anyone's control or even comprehension. Nor were all these changes due to new and unforeseen circumstances

– they related, as well, to traditional modes of thought. One such mode was the concept of pastoral power that had developed within the church and that served to individualize each member of the flock of the faithful. Another one was the deeply ingrained masculine prejudice that maintained women in a secondary and dependent position in society. Susan is able to bring out quite effectively the irony of women's situation following the onset of the Revolution, when they became known as "citoyennes." As she demonstrates by means of striking examples, the term was meaningless, because the male revolutionaries, in spite of all the rhetoric of equality, were still convinced in their heart of hearts, that woman's place was in the home – her realm was domestic and the political arena was strictly reserved for men. When Olympe de Gouges rewrote the *Declaration of the Rights of Man* in order to correct the potential male bias inherent in the document, she noted pointedly that women were fully deserving of the right to mount the scaffold as well as the speaker's rostrum. For her efforts, she was granted the first part of her wish.

A major goal for a number of Enlightenment thinkers was to elaborate a scientific understanding of the workings of the human mind. It was a purpose that eventually helped these thinkers effectuate a radical break with the biblical past and thus place such inquiries on a distinctly secular footing. It appears today that the project of emancipation was not entirely successful, however. Thus one of the standard critiques of the Enlightenment has consisted of contrasting an alleged promise of emancipation with a legacy that appears to betray the promise in fundamental ways. While the Enlightenment seemed to ensure greater freedom for the individual, it also helped set in place new kinds of subjection and repression. In other words, the truths about the nature and condition of humans that enabled the creation of new models for the self turned into the truths that eventually served to brand, control, and subject individual human beings. The inquiry into the truths governing the nature and motives of the human mind could therefore be seen as an important part of the unfinished business of the Enlightenment. The research Susan has undertaken constitutes a valuable contribution to this inquiry and sheds new light on the process of individualization begun in the eighteenth century and helps us discern some of the motives behind the process as well as its unintended consequences.

Works Cited

Foucault, Michel. *The Order of Things*. New York: Pantheon, 1970.

Rabinow, Paul, ed. *The Foucault Reader*. New York: Pantheon, 1984.

Schmidt, James, ed. *What Is Enlightenment: Eighteenth-Century Answers and Twentieth-Century Questions*. Berkeley: U of California P, 1996.

Shumway, David. *Michel Foucault*. Boston: Twayne, 1989.

Karlis Racevskis, Ph.D.
The Ohio State University

Notes on Translations

English translations of French quotes are provided for the reader in footnotes. Every attempt has been made to supply the reader with translations from a published source to facilitate the reader's own possible, further research. Where no reference is given, the translations are my own. In some cases, this was because many works cited do not have easily accessible English translations, and in other cases, I preferred my own wording. Expressions that are cognates and thus recognizable by most readers, as well as those that I paraphrased within the body of the text, are not translated into English, however.

The bibliography includes a separate section for English translations of eighteenth-century works. Where the titles of the translated works may not be apparent, the translated title is given in the footnotes at the first citation.

Works by Michel Foucault can provide challenges for the scholar wishing to quote his works in the "original language." Many of his lectures first appeared in print in the English language in edited volumes, and some works first appeared in yet another language, such as the article "Governmentality," which first appeared in print in Italian. French translations of many of his works became available only several years later. It is for these reasons that I have quoted Foucault in French in some cases, in English in others.

Acknowledgments

I would like to thank Karlis Racevskis for his guidance and valuable advice, suggestions and recommendations throughout each phase of this research project. I would also like to extend my thanks to Amanda Lucas for her assistance in locating English translations of many of the French quotes in this book. Finally, my thanks to the Seaver Research Council at Pepperdine University for providing me with a grant and fellowship to enable the completion of this book.

Chapter One

Introduction:
The Development of a New Concept of the Individual

*Si j'ai employé le mot individu, c'est qu'il m'a paru
le plus propre à indiquer les hommes de tout sexe,
de tout âge, tous membres, à mon avis,
de la grande famille qui habite le monde.*
Guyomar (1793)

At the time of the French Revolution a new way of conceptualizing the individual emerged that depended on theoretical knowledge about human nature, but also manifested itself in political practices and in the exercise of power. The concept of the individual was caught in a paradox. These practices legitimized the Revolution but also seemed to negate the individuality that the revolutionaries had claimed to celebrate. Clearly, the situation during the Revolution did not allow its participants the luxury of a strictly theoretical approach to defining the individual. They were forced to grapple with the challenges of reconciling theory with practice. As a result, the ideas concerning the individual that emerged in the last decade of the eighteenth century were not necessarily the logical outgrowth of Enlightenment thought, but were unique to the circumstances and experiences of the Revolution.

Undoubtedly, there was a connection between the Revolution and the Enlightenment that could be described not so much as a cause and effect relationship but as one of influence. As Rudolph Vierhaus explains, the Enlightenment, "belongs to the Revolution's preconditions," and it, "was made directly or indirectly responsible insofar as its abstract ideas . . . launched a process that could no longer be controlled" (337-38). The revolutionaries were influenced by the *philosophes'* abstract ideas of the individual human being that posited a hypothetical, pre-social state of nature. But as the revolutionaries tried to forge a new government and society, they were no longer able to rely on abstractions; they had to establish concrete practices based on a new, concrete definition of the individual. While the revolutionaries used ideal, abstract notions as part of the rhetoric to legitimize their actions, their attempts to enforce their ideals produced an opposing result; that is, the concrete outcomes were often contrary to the abstract, stated notions. The concept of the individual clearly reveals this contradiction.

The Revolution's development of a new definition of the individual proceeded through three major stages. First of all, conditions arose at the end of the eighteenth century making it possible to develop a concept of the individual. These conditions were inherent in the revolutionary experience. Secondly, this experience forced the acknowledgment of a new way of viewing the individual's existence that no longer depended on abstract notions and external referents that had been developed by the *philosophes*. The new way of knowing depended instead on the individual's concrete existence. This knowledge was useful for political purposes because it helped legitimize the revolutionaries' actions and ideas. The outcome of this process was paradoxical, however. While the rhetoric of the revolutionaries claimed to venerate individuals and defend their freedom from tyranny, the very notion of the individual was used to establish the authority of the revolutionaries and, in effect, to deny the freedoms they espoused in theory.

The link between establishing political power and identifying the individual is informed by Michel Foucault's thesis regarding the transition from the eighteenth to the nineteenth century. His ideas are pertinent to an investigation into this time period because he considers the end of the eighteenth century as a threshold to modernity. While numerous authors refer to Foucault in their studies on the Revolution – for example Carla Hesse, Keith Michael Baker and Roger Chartier – no one has yet applied his ideas to an in-depth study of the eighteenth century and the Revolution. Baker tries to imagine how Foucault might have accounted for the

Revolution and provides some keen observations about ways of applying Foucauldian thought to the Revolution. "Although the revolutionary period served as a key location for so many of Foucault's investigations," Baker writes in his article, "A Foucauldian French Revolution?", "he nowhere offered anything that might reasonably be called a sustained interpretation of the French Revolution as a phenomenon in itself" (188). While I will not attempt to develop what one might term a Foucauldian interpretation of the Revolution, I will use his approach as a tool for understanding the concepts that emerged from the Revolution.

The shift in an overall philosophical mode at the beginning of the nineteenth century is identified by Foucault as the discovery of finitude which denoted a transition from classical thought to modern thought. In the essay, "Qu'est-ce que les lumières?", or "What is Enlightenment?", he writes that modernity must be viewed as an attitude and as a way of relating to contemporary reality, rather than as an historical period of time (682). This idea is derived from his understanding of the way individuals perceive the world around them. In *Les Mots et les choses*, he explains how the end of the eighteenth century marked a transformation in conceptualization that signaled a departure from classical thinking – as he referred to Enlightenment thought – and ushered in a new era of knowledge strategies. Central to this shift is the development of a conception of "man." Classical thought was unable to provide an adequate definition of man in his concrete existence because the guiding principle was derived from a dimension that was transcendental to human existence – from an outside referent that was detached from life on earth:

> La pensée classique et toutes celles qui l'ont précédée [ont] pu parler de l'esprit et du corps, de l'être humain, de sa place si limitée dans l'univers, de toutes les bornes qui mesurent sa connaissance ou sa liberté, mais . . . aucune d'entre elles, jamais, n'[a] connu l'homme tel qu'il est donné au savoir moderne. L'"humanisme" de la Renaissance, le "rationalisme" des classiques ont bien pu donner une

place privilégiée aux humains dans l'ordre du monde, ils n'ont pu penser l'homme. (*Mots* 329)[1]

While Foucault consistently points to the end of the eighteenth century and beginning of the nineteenth century as the turning point in this discovery, he does not specifically locate the impetus for such a dramatic change. I propose that the process had in fact started during the time of the French Revolution. The Revolution is in fact the most obvious location for this impetus not only because of its temporal situation, but also because of the conditions created by the revolutionary experience that demanded new ways of viewing the individual.

Contrary to classical thought's abstractions of man, modern thought was able to develop an understanding that was based on the individual's concrete existence. It was able to do so because of the acceptance of the finitude of human being, or as Foucault puts it, thanks to the development of *l'analytique de la finitude*. Put another way, the legitimation of finitude established human knowledge by recognizing its very limitations. Foucault writes that "les limites de la connaissance fondent positivement la possibilité de savoir, mais dans une expérience toujours bornée, ce que sont la vie, le travail et le langage" (*Mots* 327).[2] The acknowledgment that humans are limited in their knowledge provided modern thought with the reassurance that human knowledge was reliable and valid. This analytic of finitude allowed man to realize his position as "un étrange doublet empirico-transcendantal, puisque c'est un être tel qu'on prendra en lui connaissance de ce qui rend possible

---

[1] "Classical thought, and all the forms of thought that preceded it, were able to speak of the mind and the body, of the human being, of how restricted a place he occupies in the universe, of all the limitations by which his knowledge or his freedom must be measured, but that not one of them was ever able to know man as he is posited in modern knowledge. Renaissance 'humanism' and classical 'rationalism' were indeed able to allot human beings a privileged position in the order of the world, but they were not able to conceive of man" (*Order* 318). [The English translation of *Les mots et les choses* is *The Order of Things*.]

[2] " . . . the limits of knowledge provide a positive foundation for the possibility of knowing, though in an experience that is always limited, what life, labour, and language are" (317).

toute connaissance" (329).[3] Consequently, the individual's being could no longer be defined according to a detached, exterior referent, but essentially unfolded to appear as its own referent. In other words, knowledge of the individual became self-referential and self-legitimating. An understanding of man's concrete existence provided the foundation for this modern way of thinking. Modern thought emerged when concrete forms of man's existence – man's labor ("des objets qu'il fabrique"), life ("son organisme"), and language ("ses mots") – revealed to him the finitude of self-referential definitions (324): thus, according to Foucault,

> L'expérience qui se forme au début du XIXe siècle loge la découverte de la finitude, non plus à l'intérieur de la pensée de l'infini, mais au coeur même de ces contenus qui sont donnés, par un savoir fini, comme les formes concrètes de l'existence finie. (327)[4]

Therefore, whereas classical thought was unable to conceive of man, modern thought was able to do so: "La culture moderne peut penser l'homme parce qu'elle pense le fini à partir de lui-même" (329).[5]

Foucault's writings on a notion he labels "governmentality" underscore the emergence of the individual as a modern concept, of consequence not only for the history of philosophical tendencies but also for understanding the evolution of systems of power. Foucault defined governmentality as, simply put, the art of knowing how to govern members of a given society (Gordon 7). The art of government that began developing from about the sixteenth century and into the eighteenth century became increasingly focused on the individual.[6] This mode of exercising power is "individualizing" because it is concerned with details of

---

[3] " . . . a strange empirico-transcendental doublet, since he is a being such that knowledge will be attained in him of what renders all knowledge possible" (318).
[4] "The experience taking form at the beginning of the nineteenth century situates the discovery of finitude not within the thought of the infinite, but at the very heart of those contents that are given, by a finite act of knowing, as the concrete forms of finite existence" (316).
[5] "Modern culture can conceive of man because it conceives of the finite on the basis of itself" (318).
[6] Not all historians agree with Foucault's chronology. See for example Keith Michael Baker, "A Foucauldian French Revolution?"

individual lives and activities. Foucault found that political treatises during the sixteenth century did not necessarily consist of "advice to the prince," but instead addressed the "art of government" (Governmentality 87). Characteristic of the art of governing are techniques of power that serve to direct and modify the conduct of the individuals being governed.

The development of what Foucault calls a "pastoral" kind of power illustrates this point. According to this view, the relationship between the individual and authority is derived from the Judeo-Christian metaphor of the sheep and the shepherd. The shepherd is not only concerned with the well-being of the flock as a whole, but with each individual sheep as well:

> We saw that the shepherd was to assume responsibility for the destiny of the whole flock and of each and every sheep. In the Christian conception, the shepherd must render an account – not only of each sheep, but of all their actions, all the good or evil they are liable to do, all that happens to them. (Politics and reason 68)

This pastoral power individualizes each member of the flock. Accordingly, political power gradually shifted from a focus on the affairs of the prince to an interest in the affairs of individuals within the state. This shift, Foucault notes, is indicated by an art of government that is concerned with introducing economy into affairs of the state, where economy is defined as a way of managing individuals and the affairs of the state in the same manner as a father who manages the members of his family and the affairs of his household (Governmentality 92). At the same time, political power began to develop in terms of knowing how the state might be best served by its individual members. Individuals were thus important to the state to the extent that they could contribute to serve its purposes. As Foucault puts it, "The individual becomes pertinent for the state insofar as he can do something for the strength of the state" (Political Technology 152). He contends that he is interested in analyzing not bureaucracy and administration but in "power techniques" as they apply to individuals. Graham Burchell explains Foucault's understanding of the relationship between the state and the individual by pointing out that, "Foucault focuses on the connections between ways in which individuals are politically objectified and political techniques for integrating concrete aspects of their lives and activities into the pursuit of the state's objectives" (122).

Foucault's account of modernity, as explained by David W. Bates, calls attention to the emergence of dominating and repressive institutional forms and to the development of comprehensive systems of control and observation (9). Foucault describes how an architectural design for prisons devised in the eighteenth century by Jeremy Bentham epitomized the inauguration of the exercise of power through a dominating surveillance of the individual. The panopticon was a centralized prison watch tower around which individual prison cells were constructed, so that each inmate was constantly under threat of being watched and was subjected to a permanent gaze. In *Surveiller et punir: naissance de la prison*, Foucault explains that the theme of the panopticon is "à la fois surveillance et observation . . . individualisation et totalisation" (289).[7] The prison was not only intended to punish the individual for past misdeeds, but to transform the individual. The individual was being studied and observed to the extent that knowledge about the individual was a primary objective: "Mais connaissance aussi de chaque détenu, de sa conduite, de ses dispositions profondes, de sa progressive amélioration . . . . Il faut que soient enregistrées et comptabilisées toutes les notations qu'on peut prendre sur eux" (289).[8] Power is exercised not through traditional methods of physical force, but via the act of identifying and individualizing each offender, of knowing and taking note of each person. The modern state, as demonstrated by the panopticon, was therefore becoming ever more connected with the behavior of individuals and with "identifying and codifying" them (Miller 148).

---

[7] " . . . at once surveillance and observation . . . individualization and totalization" (*Foucault Reader* 217).

[8] " . . . knowledge of each inmate, of his behavior, his deeper states of mind, his gradual improvement. . . . Every report that can be made about him must be recorded and computed" (216-17).

Not unlike Foucault, Jean-Claude Kaufmann points to the role of the modern state as he traces the history of identity and individualization, but he adds the role of modern bureaucratic exigencies to the mix. According to his thesis, an individual's identity is the result of an historic process, directed from above – that is, from the state – so that individualization is a social construct rooted in the emergence of the modern state. Central to this process was the state's need to formulate and institute a means to identify individual citizens. Kaufmann argues that the state had to invent its own world of and for administration; it needed to know, to count, and to measure those being administered in order to regulate the society (17). The state had to create *repères*, or points of reference, to facilitate the identification of individuals; hence, identity papers. His account of the history of identity papers traces how the state did not originally maintain records of personal information about individuals, but that the church was responsible for this by keeping parish registries, starting with the registration of baptisms. The practice was made obligatory in 1539 by the ordinance of Villers-Cotterêts, and evolved over the following 200 years under several additional ordinances to include marriages and burials (19). This culminated in the National Assembly's decree in 1792 that these registries be submitted by the parish priests to the municipal authorities. From this point on, identities were kept by administrative authorities. This progression was part and parcel of the modern bureaucracy and would ultimately lead to the contemporary convention of identity cards and papers, and specifically, to the national *carte d'identité* in France. He sums up this argument with the concise expression "identifier pour administrer" (18). As evidenced by the decree for parish records in 1792, the revolutionary period was at the crux of the evolution of this phenomenon where the political leaders increasingly found the need to identify the individual, and to formulate the notion of the individual citizen for the purpose of crafting the new government and society as they envisioned it. Establishing a theory of the individual, Kaufmann points out, was essential because "le nouveau système [politique] doit imaginer l'individu-citoyen pour prendre forme" (Ego 81).[9] A defining characteristic of modernity is thus that the individual must have an identity and be identifiable by others (L'invention 55).

The turning point for the notion of the individual, as both Foucault and Kaufmann assert, is therefore situated at the crossroads of classical and modern thought. The individual as an identifiable and thus controllable entity emerges with modernity, rendering the individual a *création de la modernité*, as Miguel Benasayag terms it. In *Le mythe de l'individu*, he explains that the eighteenth century inquiries into the concept of the individual were formulated in terms of a pre-social state – a way of thinking we will explore shortly. According to the classical hypothesis, the individual and community are opposing entities, where social ties are a consequence of individuals' breaking out of their isolation. Classical thought supposed that one could consider the individual on the one hand and society on the other, but the weakness of this approach, Benasayag contends, is that classical thought never questioned the conviction that individuals even existed before social ties in the first place (23). The opposition of the individual and society is false, Benasayag writes, because the individual can only be identifiable as part of a whole, or metaphorically, an atom of the mass. There can be no individual on one side and the masses on the other; where one finds the individual, one also finds the masses: "Il n'y a donc pas, d'un côté l'individu et, de l'autre, les masses. Là où l'individu se trouve, la masse se trouve aussi" (14). Benasayag also points out that the individual will claim that the self is *transhistorique*, when in fact it is not. The self is in reality not at all autonomous and separated from the world and society, and the mere suggestion that the individual is transhistorical is itself a creation of modernity (Benasayag 13). Kaufmann, too, finds fault in the idea that the individual transcends place and time. He explains that the individual identity is not only part of an historic process, it is tightly interwoven with its context: "L'individu est lui-même de la matière sociale,

---

[9] "The new [political] system must devise the citizen-individual in order to take shape."

un fragment de la société de son époque, quotidiennement fabriqué par le contexte auquel il participe" (L'invention 49).[10]

As we shall soon see, the Jacobin leaders promoted this very idea that Benasayag rejects. In their attempt to establish power, they sought to draw a line of demarcation between the individual and the masses. It is this division that enabled the revolutionaries to inaugurate a notion of the individual that ran counter to their stated ideals. On the one hand, revolutionary ideals and ideological slogans exalted the individual citizen, while on the other, the revolutionaries thrived on condemning supposed enemies of the Revolution. In other words, they had to identify individuals first in order to establish authority over them, as echoed in Kaufmann's statement *identifier pour administrer*. The individual thus functioned as a legitimizing force during the Revolution because the individuals' existence served to strengthen the revolutionaries' claim to power. "We can see," Foucault observes, "that the care for the individual life is becoming . . . a duty for the state" (Political Technology 147).

By following the evolution of the notion of the individual starting with the writings of the *philosophes* and pursuing its manifestations in the discourse and practices of the Revolution, this study adopts an interdisciplinary approach drawing from the fields of philosophy, literature, history, and political science. Both Enlightenment thought as well as Revolutionary discourse, whether written or spoken, will be viewed through a lens similar to that of literary analysis in many respects. This is not unlike the method used by other scholars of the Revolutionary period, such as François Furet and Keith Michael Baker who have engaged in an analysis of discursive practices and the importance of language therein (Landes, *Visualizing* 11). James Swenson, for another example, in his recent work on Rousseau, describes his approach as one that follows in the tradition of Lynn Hunt by employing literary criticism and applying literary techniques of reading to the

---

[10] "The individual is itself social matter, a fragment of the society of his time, created daily by the context in which he participates."

history of the French Revolution. Additionally, Caroline Weber explains that because she is studying the function of revolutionary language in *Terror and its Discontents*, she has chosen to tackle the subject as a literary scholar rather than as an historian (xx). My own approach will not depart far from that of these authors as I mine through eighteenth-century discourse to uncover notions of the individual.

The chapter that follows will begin with a survey of the ways in which Enlightenment philosophers conceptualized the individual. If we consider the end of the eighteenth century as a turning point, then we must understand what preceded it in order to appreciate its pivotal function. Eighteenth century philosophers formulated many different theories concerning governmental and political systems, and these writings will serve to provide insights into the relationship between the individual and society. We will find that they support Foucault's thesis that during the eighteenth century government was becoming increasingly interested in the individual.

The *philosophes* considered the individual in an abstract and theoretical manner, although this individual was not referred to as, "l'individu," but as, "l'homme." The definitions of "man" and of his place in the universe were not based on the individual's concrete existence but on an exterior referent. For many *philosophes,* this point of reference was nature. They tried to determine what man was in a state of pure nature, and this nature was often conceptualized in terms of a hypothetical situation in which man existed before society was organized. The first part of the chapter titled, "Enlightenment Approaches to Defining the Individual," will focus on the various ideas the *philosophes* held about nature and how these notions were used to define and describe the individual human being. Maurice Bloch and Jean H. Bloch have categorized Enlightenment meanings of nature according to four major areas in their article, "Women and the Dialectics of Nature in Eighteenth-Century French Thought." Their brief investigation of each of these areas creates an effective framework for discussing the different interpretations of nature. They note that the eighteenth century worked from a "tradition stemming from classical times

of understanding human beings in terms of a before – nature – and an after – society"
(26). They identify four different meanings of the term "nature" as it was used in
Enlightenment writings: nature can therefore be seen as 1.) a presocial state, 2.) a
functioning of the human body, which includes instincts and emotions, 3.) the co-
existence of human nature and the external world of plants and animals, and 4.) the
life of primitive peoples (27). The authors point out that these four meanings are not
necessarily separated, but are intertwined with one another. Thus, after a description
of the "before" stage, the next step is to discuss how individuals moved from a non-
social condition to one that involved an organized society. Subsequently, individuals
are defined in relation to society – in terms of their role in the formation and
functioning of society.

Definitions of this individual emerged from two schools of thought:
sensationism and materialism. Both of these relied upon the natural functioning of
the human body to describe the individual human being. John C. O'Neal's *The
Authority of Experience: Sensationist Theory in the French Enlightenment* discusses
the sensationist theory that human sense perception of external stimuli shapes each
individual's thoughts. He further distinguishes this school of thought from the
materialist concept, which argued that human beings are strictly material beings.
According to both theories, the individual human being is subject to external
influences, and is shaped by one's surroundings. O'Neal's research, along with
Duchet's *Anthropologie et histoire au siècle des lumières*, and Jean A. Perkins' *The
Concept of the Self in the French Enlightenment,* provides valuable insights regarding
these *philosophes'* ideas about the state of nature. Chapter Two thus includes an
analysis of sensationist ideas as they are found in Condillac's *Traité des sensations*,
and in Helvétius' *De l'esprit*, in addition to an examination of the materialist notions
in Morelly's *L'Essai sur l'esprit human*, La Mettrie's *L'Homme-machine,*
d'Holbach's *Système de la nature* and *Système social*, and Diderot's *Le Rêve de
d'Alembert*. The writings of d'Holbach, Helvétius, Morelly, and La Mettrie –
philosophes who are, in general, studied less frequently than Rousseau, for example

– are crucial for an understanding of the notion of the individual in the eighteenth century, yet analyses of their ideas tend to be found within larger surveys of Enlightenment philosophy, rather than in works that focus solely on their writings.

Chapter Two also examines some of the connections between these notions of the individual and the *philosophes'* theories about the formation of societies, laws and legislation. While trying to avoid an analysis that would be more suited for a political science inquiry, I will show how these abstract notions about the individual have a bearing on theories about political authority and the individual's relation to it. The progression towards an organized society ruled by law is depicted differently among the *philosophes*. Montesquieu's *De l'esprit des lois* opens with an analysis of laws that exist in a pre-social state – natural laws – and proceeds to analyze laws that develop within an established social organism – positive laws. The story of the Troglodytes in *Lettres persanes* serves as an allegory for Montesquieu's theories on the rule of law. These two works will thus be discussed at length. Shackleton's authoritative biography on Montesquieu, Merry's work, *Montesquieu's System of Natural Government*, and Goyard-Fabre's *Montesquieu: la nature, les lois, la liberté* contribute to the discussion of Montesquieu's ideas. Emile Durkheim also provides some instructive comments on Montesquieu's concept of society. These ideas lay the foundation for the revolutionaries' ideological slogans about such concepts as an individual's interests and the *volonté générale*, or the general will. While Rousseau is the main figure associated with the concept of general will, other philosophers also referred frequently to the role of the individual in relation to the society as a whole.

Helvétius, d'Holbach, Diderot, and Morelly stressed the importance of the individual in the proper functioning of society, and these works will be discussed in light of Foucault's idea that throughout the eighteenth century, governmental thought was becoming increasingly concerned with how the individual could be useful to the state by contributing to serve the state's purposes. Before the establishment of societies, individuals realized that they could more adequately fulfill their needs with the aid of others. This realization led them to assemble with others. In the resulting society, each individual therefore had to work for the good of the whole society, rather than for his or her own interest or gain. In addition to the works of Helvétius and d'Holbach, and Morelly's *Code de la nature,* various articles by Diderot, such as "Autorité politique," and "Droit naturel," will be assessed as well. Ascertaining Diderot's political ideas can be a challenging task, since, as Michèle Duchet has explained in "Diderot et 'l'Histoire des deux Indes': fragments pour une politique," Diderot was not a political thinker like Montesquieu and Rousseau, and wrote no major political text; his political ideas can be found scattered among many different works.

Rousseau's ideas concerning the individual will be treated at length. The portion of the chapter devoted to Rousseau will include an investigation of his concept of nature and how it relates to his understanding of society, the individual, and government. The discussion begins with a study of Rousseau's state of nature and the origins of society as found in *Discours sur l'inégalité* and *Essai sur l'origine des langues.* I will examine Rousseau's notion of the individual in a pre-social state, as well as in the social state – one that is, according to Rousseau, an unnatural entity. *Emile* presents an individual in the latter situation, and provides important insights into Rousseau's concept of the individual. Crocker's *The Prophetic Voice* is particularly informative here because of his understanding of Emile as a "reconstructed individual." The pupil is reconstructed through the teachings of his tutor, in the same way that members of society in *Economie politique* are to be formed by their government. The reconstructed individual is thus prepared to live in the "reconstructed society," as Crocker terms it, that is conceptualized in *Du contrat social.*

Chapter Three, "The French Revolution's Struggle to Reconcile the Abstract Individual and the Concrete Individual," provides a thorough analysis of the conditions during the revolutionary years of 1789 to 1794 that made it possible to develop a new conception of the individual. These conditions involved the concrete experience of forging a new form of government and society. An important characteristic of the Revolution was its dependence on many abstract notions that established unattainable ideals. The concept of the individual played a vital role in revolutionary rhetoric, but the rhetoric did not always express the tangible reality associated with this concept. Yet this rhetoric did serve to legitimize the revolutionaries' actions. The revolutionaries soon learned – whether they were aware of the paradox or not – that while they depended on abstract definitions of the individual, they could not rely on them as practical guides for exercising power. They were therefore faced with the reality of people's concrete existence, which, as Foucault argued, became a foremost concern for the state.

The third chapter begins with an assessment of the concepts of sovereignty and general will. Rousseau criticized the idea that sovereignty resided in one specific individual and claimed instead that sovereignty dwelled in a general public will that expressed the sum of individual interests. Thus the many individuals are fused to become the sovereign nation, or as Daniel Roche explains, the *Contrat social* describes, "une politique où tous les individus se fondent et se pensent comme individu" (486).[11] By definition the general will had to be a unified will, and consequently, sovereignty depended on the indivisibility of the people. As Baker explains, "Unity was the condition of sovereignty" (Sovereignty 856). Individuals were the requisite foundation of sovereignty but any individual that seemed to express an interest that was contrary to the presumed general will was viewed with suspicion and distrust. Liberty for the individual was assured only as long as his private interests conformed to those of an abstract, general will. Therefore, the individual's interests were pitted against the general will.

The concept of sovereignty is an abstract notion, whereas the individual being is concrete and tangible. National sovereignty exists in the rights-bearing individual, but if the individual does not become fused with someone else's idea of the people's will, that individual becomes an enemy to the sovereign nation. Such enemies paid

---

[11] "... a political system where all individuals merge together and think as one."

the price of their difference at the guillotine; the concrete was punished in the name of the abstract. As Peter Brooks explains it: "when . . . abstractions are translated into actions, people are to live or die as a consequence of rhetorical moves" (35). The trial of the king demonstrates the process by which individuals were rhetorically eliminated from the unified citizenry before being physically eliminated. The Revolution's leaders portrayed the king as an outsider to the French people, and as exterior to the social contract. This type of portrayal would be used repeatedly to describe the Revolution's adversaries. Speeches by Robespierre and Saint-Just emphasize the opposition of wills, as do those of Billaud-Varenne, another member of the Committee of Public Safety, who made noteworthy remarks on the distinction between the individual and the citizen.

Enemies had to be identified as individuals whose private interest posed a threat to the unity of the people. Their individual, private will had to be exposed in order to protect the *patrie*. I will survey the various means by which individual foes were identified and declared enemies drawing from legal documents such as the Law of Suspects and the Law of 22 Prairial, and from documents relating to institutional apparatuses, including the Revolutionary Tribunal and the watch committees. Speeches by Danton, Robespierre, and Saint-Just and the writings of Marat also establish the imperative to identify the individual as a source of discord. Marat in particular was famous for his incessant denunciations of individuals whom he deemed counterrevolutionary and traitorous.

The chapter concludes with an analysis of virtue as it was defined within a political context. Robespierre drew heavily on Rousseau's concept of virtue and sought to make this concept consistent with reality. He yearned for a republic where each individual loved the nation and its laws, and contributed to the well being of the *patrie*. He discovered, however, that individuals were not all virtuous; the abstract "people," on the other hand, was to be considered pure and virtuous. As a result of this dichotomy, he rhetorically expelled individuals from his understanding of the people.

Chapter Three draws heavily from primary sources on the Revolution, particularly from the *Archives parlementaires,* the *Réimpression de l'ancien Moniteur* (a journal that first appreared in 1789), and transcriptions of speeches by leaders such as Robespierre and Saint-Just. Recent scholarly research also provides vital insights into the concept of the individual, such as that of Lucien Jaume's *Le Discours jacobin et la démocratie,* Carol Blum and Baker which are used throughout the chapter. Jaume's work on Jacobin discourse includes an analysis of the ambiguous role of the individual within this discourse. He explains, "Tantôt qu'il apparaît par excès de positivité, tantôt parce qu'il ne se confond pas avec l'unité requise par les principes, 'l'individu' reste une catégorie énigmatique à l'intérieur du discours des Jacobins" (179).[12] Baker also sheds light on the relationship between the individual and sovereignty in his article, "A Foucauldian French Revolution?" where he describes this relationship within a Foucauldian framework. Blum's *Rousseau and the Republic of Virtue* informs the discussion on the virtuous individual, with its useful insights into revolutionary rhetoric – including, but not exclusively Jacobin rhetoric, as does George Rudé and Palmer's respective studies on Robespierre and R. R. Palmer's *Twelve Who Ruled.*

The fourth chapter explores the particular case of women since their experience provides a clear example of the problems associated with reconciling theory with practice. The role to which women were relegated during the Revolution indicates a certain distrust of the individual's – in this case, female's – "contenus qui sont donnés [les mots, l'organisme, le travail] comme les formes concrètes de l'existence finie" (Foucault, *Mots* 327).[13] As the experience of the Revolution inevitably led to the discovery of an individual's concrete existence that was often opposed to its abstract representation, it also created glaring contradictions in the case

---

[12] "At times he appears with an excess of positivity, and at other times he does not conform to the unity required by their principles; so 'the individual' remains an enigmatic category within Jacobin discourse."
[13] ". . . contents that are given [language, life, and labor], by a finite act of knowing, as the concrete forms of finite existence" (316).

of female citizens. While national sovereignty was said to reside in the individual, this individual was assumed to be male rather than female. Joan Wallach Scott explains: "For women, the legacy of the French Revolution was contradictory: a universal, abstract, rights-bearing individual as the unit of national sovereignty, embodied, however, as a man" (1). Orators espoused the idea that all individuals were born with natural rights, while in practice, women were discouraged from participating politically. But women forged ahead and took the initiative to participate in many political events and to speak in various political forums. At the same time, women were discouraged from participating in these public political activities, unless their participation conformed to the ideals of domestic, private virtue. It is clear that during the Revolution, these attitudes had to confront the concrete political involvement of many women as well as the rhetoric of freedom and equality, and this confrontation created new practices and revised definitions.

Early in the revolutionary period Olympe de Gouges, Condorcet, and the Cercle Social published writings that reacted to the apparent promise of equality and expressed enthusiastic and optimistic support for women's political rights. Condorcet, basing his argument on women's capacity to reason as human beings, urged that women be permitted the right to vote. The Cercle Social and Olympe de Gouges also argued that the political individual – referred to as "*l'homme*" in the *Déclaration des droits de l'homme* – was not, in fact, a gender-specific being. This chapter, "The Female Individual and the French Revolution," includes reflections on the ambiguous term, "man"/"*l'homme*," and the unequivocal term, "woman"/"*femme*," while analyzing the Revolution's apparent promise that individual rights would be granted universally to all individuals.

The question of citizenship was, in many ways, at the heart of the debate concerning women. Etta Palm d'Aelders, Théroigne de Méricourt, Pauline Léon, and Claire Lacombe actively pursued women's participation in the political arena by making numerous public speeches and organizing women's political associations. The Club des Citoyennes Républicaines Révolutionnaires, was one such female political club that aggressively claimed that the Revolution intended for women to be veritable citizens of the sovereign nation. While many male political leaders did not hesitate to refer to women as *citoyennes*, they denied women the rights that were granted to male citizens. Godineau notes the contradiction of a female citizen who does not enjoy rights of citizenship. She refers to women as, "cet individu étrange qu'est une citoyenne sans citoyenneté" (*Citoyennes* 113).[14] Chapter Four surveys some of the notions of citizenship as they related to the particular issue of women's citizenship. Godineau's observations on the meanings of citizenship in her article, "Autour du mot *citoyenne*," is an indispensable resource for this discussion. As the Revolution progressed, it became increasingly clear that women were not to be included in definitions of the rights-bearing individual. By the end of 1793, the denial of women as equal, individual citizens was firmly established. Furthermore, women were clearly called to demonstrate a specifically female virtue of domesticity, whereas men were exhorted to a public, political virtue. In order to justify this distinction, many revolutionary leaders – similar to the Enlightenment thinkers before them – referred to the limitations that nature supposedly imposed upon women. According to this reasoning, nature gave women physical characteristics that determined their domestic, maternal functions and excluded them from public, political functions. Orators and writers such as Prudhomme, Hérault de Séchelles, Chaumette, and Amar used this argument to denounce women's political activity and to refuse women the rights of citizens. Their writings and speeches, as well as a pivotal debate in the Convention in the fall of 1793, will be closely examined in Chapter Four.

There has been an abundance of works in recent years regarding women during the Revolution. Levy, Applewhite, and Johnson's collection of English translations of revolutionary speeches and writings by and about women is a valuable resource, the French versions of which are found primarily in *Les Femmes dans la*

---

[14] " . . . this strange individual who is a citizen without citizenship."

Révolution Française. Applewhite and Levy have collaborated on several articles that discuss the revolutionary experience for women, and have edited an informative collection of essays in *Women and Politics in the Age of the Democratic Revolution.* Scholars such as Joan Wallach Scott, in "French Feminists and the Rights of 'Man'," as well as in *Only Paradoxes to Offer,* and Suzanne Desan's, "Women's Experience of the French Revolution," suggest that the Revolution was contradictory for women and sent them mixed messages. Scott's work on Olympe de Gouges and the more recent *Only Paradoxes* carefully explain the Revolution's contradictory experience for women. I will also refer to Dominique Godineau's examination of the women of Paris during the Revolution and her analysis of citizenship found in, *Citoyennes Tricoteuses: Les Femmes du peuple à Paris pendant la Révolution française.* Marie Cerati's research on the Club des Citoyennes, and Gary Kates' article on the Cercle Social are important for their discussion of specific organizations that promoted women's rights. *Rebel Daughters: Women and the French Revolution,* a collection of articles edited by Sara E. Melzer and Leslie W. Rabine, has also provided important contributions to the field.

The chapter concludes with some reflections on the results of the clashes between rhetoric, allegory and political practice. The revolutionary experience ultimately rejected women's individuality. In order for women to be permitted to participate fully in the rights of citizenship, they would have to be recognized as individuals endowed with the same natural rights as men. But the universality of rights was rejected. The *Déclaration des droits de l'homme et du citoyen* was ultimately interpreted as a declaration of inalienable rights for male individuals only.

A fundamental difficulty in investigating the notion of the individual is determining who, precisely, is implied when one refers to individual human beings with masculine nouns and pronouns. The use of the word, "*l'homme,*" or "man," is problematic since the term could be understood to mean humanity in general or to designate an individual male human being. When the *philosophes* were hypothesizing about the individual, were they deliberately referring to a male human being, or did they have both man and woman in mind? Were their discussions focused on a gender-neutral human capacity or a strictly masculine one? Similarly, did the *Déclaration des droits de l'homme et du citoyen* intentionally leave all references to the individual in the masculine forms to imply the exclusion of women? Or was it merely the linguistic rule of thumb in French that dictates masculine forms to refer to both men and women? These ambiguities are fundamental aspects of the Revolution's mixed messages concerning women, and present complications for our own understanding of eighteenth-century intentions as well.

We are additionally confronted with the difficult task of knowing how to discuss these ideas and express them appropriately and accurately with today's language tools. In other words, should we parallel their ambiguous use of "man," remaining faithful to the original terminology, but risk leaving our own discussion equally unclear? Or should we adopt contemporary rules for gender-neutral language,[15] but risk leaving the impression that eighteenth-century texts and speeches were intended to be gender-neutral? To resolve this dilemma, I have chosen to employ gender-neutral language in most cases because doing so will retain the ambiguity of the original texts. A current trend for nonsexist language that I will not implement, however, is the use of both female and male pronouns interchangeably.[16] When paraphrasing a writer I will occasionally replicate the use of "man" and of similar expressions but my aim is to avoid this whenever possible. Finally, Chapter Four explores this very issue in detail, and the discussion of the meanings of the individual will not be an undercurrent as in the preceding chapters, but will be confronted head-on.

---

[15] There are many guides on how to adopt a gender-neutral writing style. See for example *Language, Gender, and Professional Writing* by Francine Wattman Frank et al.
[16] Paul Olivier suggests this practice: "Sometimes, the use of a pronoun will be alternated, using 'he' in one chapter of a section, 'she' in the next section, followed by reversion to 'he'" (67).

Chapter Two

Enlightenment Approaches to Defining the Individual

Ils n'ont pu penser l'homme.
Foucault (1966)

When the French Enlightenment philosophers spoke of individual human beings and of their place in the universe, they did so in terms of a guiding principle that was detached from humans' concrete existence. Rather than referring to the concrete forms of human existence that are discussed by Foucault – life, labor, and language – the *philosophes* referred to individuals as they are posited in nature. In the eighteenth century nature gained the distinction of providing the theoretical framework for understanding human beings. The state of nature was conceptualized in a variety of ways throughout the century and, consequently, led to various conclusions and to new questions as well. Ehrard has observed that during the first half of the century, nature was viewed with unparalleled enthusiasm: "Au temps de Montesquieu . . . la majorité des esprits cultivés inclinent à accorder à la nature une confiance inconditionnelle. Elle est partout, envahit tout" (421).[1] But during the second half of the century nature underwent a more critical analysis. Ehrard explains that, "Après 1750 les choses seront moins simples. Le règne de la nature sera à la fois plus voyant et moins incontesté . . . . Entre 1760 et 1780 la Nature posera autant de questions qu'elle en résoudra" (422).[2] As the end of the century approached, the precise nature of the individual remained unresolved.

---

[1] "During the time of Montesquieu . . . the majority of learned minds tended to accord an unconditional trust in nature. Nature is everywhere, pervades everything."
[2] "After 1750 things were less simple. The reign of Nature was at once more strident and less uncontested . . . . Between 1760 and 1780 Nature posed as many questions as it answered."

Sensationism, materialism and nature

One tendency among the Enlightenment philosophers such as Condillac, La Mettrie, Helvétius and d'Holbach, was the consideration of the individual according to the natural functioning of the human body. In their analyses the meaning of the term "nature" focused on the operations of the human body, which consisted primarily of sense perception and the ability to process the information received through the senses. By viewing nature in this manner, these philosophers developed notions of the human being in terms of such frames of reference as sensationism[3] and materialism, notions whereby the individual being was seen to exist as a sort of mechanism. While materialism and sensationism are similar in that they are both a consequence and a manifestation of a particular view of nature, they differ on the connection between mind and matter. Sensationist theory asserted that ideas were ultimately derived from human sensations, whereas materialists believed that the origin of ideas were to be located in matter and its movement (O'Neal 198). In this latter view, the senses serve to transmit the original information. In both theories, however, ideas are not innate but are formed internally as a result of circumstances that are external to the individual being.

No longer satisfied with the Cartesian doctrine of, *Je pense, donc je suis*, Enlightenment philosophers questioned human knowledge, and the individual's senses and sensations provided the answer to this inquiry. Human nature could be ascertained by referring to the operation of the senses, whose function was part and parcel of the natural processes of the body. The *philosophe* Etienne Bonnot de Condillac adhered to this emphasis on the senses and was influential in establishing sensationism as a rule for human understanding. In *Traité des sensations* (1754), Condillac clearly expresses the ideas that are central to sensationism by pointing out that sensations are inextricably linked to an individual's capacity to compare, judge,

---

[3] John C. O'Neal, in *The Authority of Experience*, prefers the use of the term "sensationism" to avoid confusion with the journalistic connotation of the term "sensationalism." For his discussion of the terms, see his introduction. I will follow O'Neal's terminology as well.

reflect, and remember. These operations of the mind are subordinate to sensation (O'Neal 18-19). He explains this relationship in the following manner: "Le jugement, la réflexion, les passions, toutes les opérations de l'âme, en un mot, ne sont que la sensation même qui se transforme différemment" (14).[4] These operations of sense perception constitute the individual's psychological reality (Cassirer 25). The individual's thinking capacity is a result of the experiences to which one's senses are exposed; the senses process this information in a way that forms thoughts. Condillac remarks, "La sensation après avoir été attention, comparaison, jugement, devient donc encore la réflexion même" (19).[5] Human consciousness is thus shaped by the external stimuli that individuals sense. Human nature makes each individual capable of forming ideas based on the reception of impressions that are acquired from objects in the universe. Sensationism stresses the extent to which humans are completely shaped by sensory acquisition and experience.

Condillac's influence on Helvétius is apparent in *De l'esprit*, where Helvétius argues in favor of the theories of sensationism. He asserts that physical sensitivity is the foundation for the human mind and predisposes it to acquire knowledge. Yet he carries these ideas further by attributing everything in humanity to physical sensibility: pleasure, pain, virtue, vice, self-interest and sociability (O'Neal 84). Along with other sensationists, he bases his analysis on the idea that humans are born without ideas and therefore are neither naturally good nor evil. The influence of a Lockean *tabula rasa* is evident here, a concept according to which the mind is blank at birth but is able to record impressions through the senses. The individual's experiences shape the mind and consequently, as Helvétius argues, the mind is the result of acquired sense perceptions. The individual is thus defined according to a process of coupling external stimuli with natural, internal faculties of the brain. Helvétius explains in *De l'esprit* that the first factor in this process is our physical

---

[4] "Judgment, reflection, and passions – all operations of the mind are, in a word, only the sensation itself which is transformed differently."
[5] "Sensations, after having been attention, comparison, and judgment, become the reflection itself."

sensitivity, which enables us to receive impressions of what is external to us (71). This ability, which he refers to as "sensibilité physique," enables the second faculty – memory – to sustain the impression. These two faculties in conjunction produce thoughts. Condillac had stressed that memory played a vital role in human reflection as well, and thus an insight in *De l'esprit* closely parallels that of Condillac. Condillac explained that, "La mémoire n'est donc que la sensation transformée" (17)[6], whereas Helvétius described memory as, "une sensation continuée, mais affaiblie" (71).[7]

While both memory and physical sensitivity are natural and distributed equally among all individuals, not all individuals are able to make equal use of the mind, however. The mind for Helvétius must process the ideas that have been acquired, and this operation is the ability to make judgments. This basic function serves to differentiate between objects as well as to find similarities: "C'est dans la capacité que nous avons d'apercevoir les ressemblances ou les différences, les convenances ou les disconvenances qu'ont entre eux les objets divers, que consistent toutes les opérations de l'esprit" (77).[8] In other words, all operations of the mind boil down to judgment. Yet the inequality between the judgments of different individuals is a result not of any natural inequality, but of differences in environmental factors. While Helvétius writes of the "inégale capacité d'attention des hommes" in the third discourse of *De l'esprit*, he explains that this is dependent on the external conditions within which each individual lives. He stresses the importance of the environment's influence. In fact, the individual is molded not by the internal workings of the mind but by the accumulation of sense perceptions and the differentiation of these impressions. Environmental conditions determine, therefore, the personality of the

---

[6] "Memory is nothing but transformed sensation."

[7] " . . . a continued, but weakened, sensation" (2).

[8] " . . . that all the operations of the Mind consist in the power we have of perceiving the resemblance and difference, the agreement or disagreement, of various objects among themselves" (7).

individual. If all ideas are acquired and are neither innate nor natural, then individuals are defined by what is external to their own human existence.

Like sensationist theories, materialist theories contended that individuals were formed by external conditions, but the latter theory stressed a monistic, rather than dualistic, conception of human beings (O'Neal 204). Materialism was contrary to the Cartesian tradition of the duality of the self, a notion comprising both mind and body. These philosophers were unsatisfied with the Cartesian and Christian idea of an entity that is at once unified and separate, and is identified with the soul (J. Perkins 41). According to materialists, the mind and body are one and there is no duality; the human being is not formed of two distinct entities. The soul is merely another material feature of the human body, as described by Julien Offray de La Mettrie in *L'Homme-machine*: "Toutes les facultés de l'âme dépendent tellement de la propre organisation du cerveau & de tout le corps, qu'elles ne sont visiblement que cette organisation même" (330)[9]. The soul, like all aspects of the human being, consists of matter, and it is this matter that defines and precedes the senses (O'Neal 203). In short, it is the physical qualities of human beings that constitute the nature of the individual, according to d'Holbach whose *Système de la nature* authoritatively defines the materialist standpoint. He perceives the human being as a purely physical, material object. His strict and succinct characterization of the individual reveals the extent to which human beings are made up of physical qualities exclusively. "L'homme est un être purement physique," he writes (*Système de la Nature* 3)[10],[11]. Because of these purely physical attributes, a human is subject to the laws of nature that are composed primarily of the movement of matter. He begins *Système de la nature* by establishing nature as the basis of all that constitutes the human being: "L'homme est l'ouvrage de la nature, il existe dans la nature, il est

---

[9] "All the faculties of the soul depend so much on the proper organization of the brain and the entire body, since these faculties are obviously just this organized brain itself" (59).
[10] *Système de la nature* will henceforth be abbreviated *SN*; *Système social* will be abbreviated *SS*.
[11] "Man is a purely physical being."

soumis à ses lois, il ne peut s'en affranchir, il ne peut, même par la pensée, en sortir" (1-2).[12] Each individual, being an integral part of nature, is unable to stand apart from it. Nature has organized the human body in such a way that it is incapable of acting contrary to that which nature has prescribed. The individual is not a privileged being in nature but is subject to changes and movement within the universe, as are all material things. He writes, "l'homme . . . n'agit jamais que d'après les lois propres à son organisation et aux matières dont la nature l'a composé" (*SN* 5)[13], and mocks the idea that human beings can overcome the strict dictates of the laws of nature. The sixth chapter of *Système de la nature* criticizes those who believe that any individual can be superior to nature: "Toi qui dans ta folie prends arrogamment le titre de Roi de la nature! . . . l'homme n'a point de raisons pour se croire un être privilégié dans la nature" (105, 107).[14] All individuals are products of the same universal nature and thus, each individual is identified not by one's own life, language and labor – to use Foucault's terms – but by one's relationship with the external world.

The role of the external world on an individual's senses was underscored by Morelly in *L'Essai sur l'esprit humain*. Human beings, he claimed, are born with physical workings of the body that have no other functions than, "ceux qui sont communs à toute machine" (qtd. in Chinard 12).[15] Morelly writes that external objects affect individuals first by stirring up the workings of the mind – *l'esprit* – and intellect, and setting into motion the functions of imagination, memory, reflection, and judgment. Secondly, these sensations give rise to internal feelings – in "notre *coeur*" – of what is pleasant or unpleasant. Morelly concludes, "On peut donc définir physiquement *l'esprit* par *les mouvemens combinés des organes en tant qu'ils*

---

[12] "He is the work of nature. He exists in Nature. He is submitted to the laws of Nature. He cannot deliver himself from them: cannot step beyond them even in thought" (1).

[13] "Man . . . never acts but according to the laws peculiar to his organization, and to the matter of which he is composed" (4).

[14] "You, who in your folly, arrogantly assume to yourself the title of King of Nature! . . . man has no solid reason to believe himself a privileged being in Nature."

[15] " . . . those that are common to all machines."

s'agissent sur l'intellect" (qtd. in Chinard 13).[16]   Ideas are not innate but are
produced by the senses.

The universality of human nature, described in *Système social*, renders
individuals indistinguishable from one another, although the effects of what exists
independently of them does allow for some differentiation. "L'homme est partout
le même," he writes, and humans therefore have

> une même nature; les différences que l'on trouve entre eux ne sont
> que des modifications de cette même nature, produites par le climat,
> le gouvernement, l'éducation, les opinions, & par les différentes
> causes qui agissent sur eux. Les hommes ne diffèrent que dans les
> idées qu'ils se font du bonheur. (*SS* I: 56, 57)[17]

Like Helvétius, d'Holbach stresses the influence of education and society – external
forces – on the individual's thoughts. In accordance with sensationism, ideas come
not from within human beings, but are formed through the sense reception of external
stimuli. For materialists, on the other hand, the senses are merely one part of the
body's mechanism that responds to stimuli and do not play quite the same role in
forming thoughts as they do for sensationists. For sensationists, ideas originate with
the senses, but for materialists, the original source for ideas rests with movement of
matter. O'Neal describes d'Holbach's interpretation of matter this way:

> D'Holbach connects the senses to matter in such a way that the latter
> ultimately governs the former deterministically rather than interacts
> with them in a way that might lead one to believe that the senses can
> act independently. (200)

It is the functioning of the brain that processes the sensations, so that an idea is only
an imperceptible modification of the brain (*SN* 197).

---

[16] "One can therefore define the mind as 'the combined movement of the organs as they act upon the
intellect'."

[17] "Man is the same everywhere . . . [and all humans have] the same nature; the differences that are
found between them are only modifications of this nature, products of the climate, government,
education, opinions, and the different causes that act on them. Men differ from one another only in
their ideas of what will lead to their happiness."

According to d'Holbach and the other philosophers who subscribed to materialist theses, ideas are not inherent in the essential character of the individual, but are the effects of movement in the universe. Materialists rejected the notion that matter had no inherent action or motion. Matter was inherently active and in constant motion, and this quality of matter was essential to the cognitive process. La Mettrie had written in *L'Homme-machine* that "l'âme n'est qu'un principe de mouvement" (339).[18] Diderot would agree that movement is an integral part of human existence and had in fact examined the individual from the same materialist perspective as d'Holbach and La Mettrie. Diderot considered individual human beings as one part of the material universe, rather than an entity to be considered in isolation from it (J. Perkins 118).

Diderot develops the materialist notion that human beings are made up of organized matter, as are all things in the universe. *Le Rêve de d'Alembert* takes on the difficult task of explaining an organization of the universe where sensitive elementary particles form the basic building blocks for all matter, including human beings.[19] To this notion of a basic structure, Diderot adds the principle of movement, implying a principle of change. Movement is inherent in all matter, even in the smallest particles. Sensitivity, which is characteristic of all particles, produces a certain energy which is latent in inanimate objects, and active in animate objects (J. Perkins 119). All matter in the physical world is thus in a state of continual flux: "Tout est en un flux perpétuel" (Diderot, *Rêve* 899).[20]

The individual elements of the universe cannot be isolated from each other. Instead, they form a continuous chain that makes up the whole. Within this whole

---

[18] "The soul is only a principle of movement" (65).

[19] Arthur M. Wilson compares these particles to a cell, which had not yet been discovered in Diderot's time (562).

[20] This continual movement produces an important justification for determinism and causality in materialist thought. As a result, human beings are subject to the determinism of movement. As O'Neal explains, "Materialism dwarfs the importance of humanity by subjecting it and everything else to the material world's laws of causality" (213). Individuals lose, in effect, much of their identity as singular, unique beings.

entity, however, individual units can be discerned. Smaller parts combine with others to form aggregates which are then subject to what J. Perkins calls a principle of organization which takes over and determines this new unit (119). Diderot uses the image of a swarm of bees to make this point. While a swarm of bees appears as a single unit, it is in fact composed of an aggregate of parts – individual bees – that contribute to the whole swarm. Individual human beings are likewise one small part of the whole universe. Diderot describes the unity of the whole of nature and goes so far as to say there are no individuals, but only the whole, or the "seul grand individu":

> Ne convenez-vous pas que tout tient en nature et qu'il est impossible qu'il y ait un vide dans la chaîne? Que voulez-vous donc dire avec vos individus? Il n'y en a point... Il n'y a qu'un seul grand individu, c'est le tout. (*Rêve* 899)[21]

The whole cosmos is one unified body, and as O'Neal puts it, human beings are one link in the Chain of Being (213).

Diderot was also attracted to a concept of nature that was represented by the lives of primitive peoples and exotic cultures. This particular interpretation of nature was not uncommon in eighteenth-century writings. Rather than viewing primitive societies as inferior to "civilized" societies, some *philosophes* considered them as a model for what was to be considered natural. The life of primitives – whether real or imaginary – was described in detail in order to demonstrate what the writers deemed as the most natural people, as opposed to contemporary society which, by comparison, had supposedly strayed from what was natural to humans. The characteristics of primitive peoples provided the foundation and furnished a referent for analyzing human nature.

---

[21] "Don't you agree that in nature everything is bound up with everything else, and that there cannot be a gap in the chain? Then what are you talking about with your individuals? There is no such thing. ... There is but one great individual, and that is the whole" (181).

This view is developed in Diderot's *Supplément au voyage de Bougainville*, a narrative that is indicative of the Enlightenment philosopher's fascination with the exotic. Diderot provides a fictitious account of a Tahitian society whose members are ruled not by laws created by humans, but by the laws of nature. They are free to express their bodily instincts and impulses, a Tahitian elder says to Bougainville: "Nous suivons le pur instinct de la nature" (970).[22] Goodman argues that although Diderot presents a comparison between this primitive and natural society in Tahiti and the contemporary French society, he does not necessarily conclude that the Tahitian man is more natural than the French man. According to Diderot, Goodman writes, "All men are natural, but civilized man is unable to act naturally toward other men because it is his society that legislates how he is to act" (133-34). Diderot suggests that laws which restrict human instinct necessarily restrict individuals from fulfilling their roles as complete human beings. The Tahitian Orou says to the French chaplain, "Ton premier devoir est d'être homme" (976).[23] The trappings of a legislated society prevent individuals from exercising their natural inclinations and duties to their physical drives.

The individual and society

In addition to attempting to define the individual, the *philosophes* also had to grapple with the issue of the individual's relationship with organized society. They tended to consider the individual as an active member of society whose role was to contribute to its effective functioning. One common factor among these philosophical considerations was a notion of the progression from a non-social existence to a social one. Involved in this development was legislation and the concept of a contract which brought order and organization to the association of individuals. This evolution is conceived differently by the various Enlightenment

---

[22] "We follow the pure instincts of nature" (*Political Writings* 42). Diderot's essays and articles appearing in the collection, *Political Writings*, will henceforth be reference with the abbreviation *PW*.
[23] "Your first duty is to be a man" (*PW* 47).

thinkers, however, and Montesquieu, for example, differs from the others by refusing to theorize in depth about the origins of society. While in *De l'esprit des lois* (1748) he does discuss the state of nature, the laws that ensue are of more interest to him than the question of how the society formed in the first place. The 94th letter of the *Lettres persanes* (1721) conveys a short and concise description of his version of the origin of society: "[Les hommes] naissent tous liés les uns aux autres; un fils est né auprès de son père, et il s'y tient: voilà la société et la cause de la société" (111).[24] Quite simply, children are born dependent on their parents and this dependence creates a familial and inseparable association that organizes the first societies. Nevertheless, his brief discussion of the origin of societies in *De l'esprit des lois* differs slightly from the account in *Lettres persanes*. This disparity is due to the fact that in *De l'esprit des lois*, Montesquieu was conforming to the established style of political treatises of his time by examining the individual in the absence of political power in the state of nature (Merry 1-2). In the first book of *De l'esprit des lois*, Montesquieu begins his discussion of laws and their relation to society by first pointing to the laws of nature: "Avant toutes ces lois, sont celles de la nature," he explains, "Pour les connaître bien, il faut considérer un homme avant l'établissement des sociétés" (531).[25] In Montesquieu's state of nature, individuals felt weak, fearful, and inferior to others, and were inclined to be most concerned with their self-preservation and nourishment. Rather than fighting with others to meet their physical needs, as Thomas Hobbes asserted, they naturally associated with them when they realized that the fear was mutual. Montesquieu disagreed on this point with Hobbes, calling Hobbes' assertion unreasonable:

> Le désir que Hobbes donne d'abord aux hommes de se subjuguer les
> uns les autres, n'est pas raisonnable. . . . La crainte porterait les

---

[24] "They are born dependent upon each other. The son comes into the world beside his father and stays there, and this is both the definition and the cause of society" (155).
[25] "Prior to all these laws are the laws of nature . . . . To know them well, one must consider a man before the establishment of societies" (6).

hommes à se fuir: mais les marques d'une crainte réciproque les engageraient bientôt à s'approcher. (*Esprit* 531)[26]

Hobbes had insisted that fear made individuals aggressive towards others, and that they were therefore naturally engaged in war rather than in sociability. Montesquieu on the other hand, noted that peace, not conflict, was the first natural law: "On ne chercherait donc point à s'attaquer, et la paix serait la première loi naturelle" (*Esprit* 531).[27] Individuals quickly discovered that a state of mutual dependence was beneficial to them, and it was this interdependence that established the basis of society. Individuals associate with others not through the exercise of force or by a prior contract, but by the desire to live in association with one another. And in doing so, they are in fact conforming to a fundamental, natural law. Once society has been established, each individual loses the prior sense of weakness and eventually enters into conflict with others, both within the society as well as with other societies. "Ces deux sortes d'état de guerre font établir les lois parmi les hommes," Montesquieu concludes (*Esprit* 531).[28] Such laws exist because of the natural progression of human existence whereby individuals move into a social state because of the natural, innate tendency toward sociability. Subsequently, competition and aggression appear among individuals, and finally laws are created serving to maintain social order by controlling aggression between people, and between governed and governors. Positive laws serve to govern society as individuals adopt an aggressive or disruptive behavior.[29]

Laws that develop within these associations are directly linked to the individuals that form them, and are furthermore based on natural law. The definition

---

[26] "Hobbes gives men first the desire to subjugate one another, but this is not reasonable . . . fear would lead men to flee one another, but the marks of mutual fear would soon persuade them to approach one another" (6).

[27] "Such men would not seek to attack one another, and peace would be the first natural law" (6).

[28] "These two sorts of states of war bring about the establishment of laws among men" (7).

[29] Goyard-Fabre has noted the influence of the seventeenth century philosopher, Jean Domat, on Montesquieu's thought in this regard. A friend of Pascal, Domat wrote in *Traité des lois* that, "La société a besoin de lois qui règlent et la conduite de chacun en particulier et l'ordre de la société qu'ils forment ensemble" (qtd. in Goyard-Fabre 74).

of law that opens *De l'esprit des lois* demonstrates that laws are not arbitrary but are a consequence of the nature of things. Montesquieu begins his work by stating, "Les lois, dans la signification la plus étendue, sont les rapports nécessaires qui dérivent de la nature des choses" (*Esprit* 530).[30] Montesquieu distinguishes two types of laws that are both derived from nature, albeit from two different manifestations of this nature. First are the laws of nature, which as described above, are laws that exist in a pre-social state, and include the laws of self-preservation, procreation, peace, and sustenance. On the other hand, the laws that relate to society, which are Montesquieu's primary concern in *De l'esprit des lois*, are derived from the nature of the physical environment, the nature of the people, and the social organism (Durkheim 21).

The most natural laws and forms of government for a particular society depend on the unique characteristics – the geography, the climate, the *moeurs*, the religion – that compose the particular social organism. This principle of relativity, for which *De l'esprit des lois* is perhaps best known, is expressed in the third chapter: "Il vaut mieux dire que le gouvernement le plus conforme à la nature est celui dont la disposition particulière se rapporte mieux à la disposition du peuple pour lequel il est établi" (*Esprit* 532).[31] The establishment of such laws would not be possible without the will of all the individuals: "Les forces particulières ne peuvent se réunir sans que toutes les volontés se réunissent" (*Esprit* 532).[32] As a consequence of this union of wills, the laws must correspond to the nature and character of those who constitute it. Montesquieu avoids, nevertheless, a discussion of the individual's rights or obligations within the society. *De l'esprit des lois* reveals little about Montesquieu's thought on the rights of individuals, although it does attack indolence and passivity as they related to social activity (Merry 29). Durkheim finds that

---

[30] "Laws, taken in the broadest meaning, are necessary relations deriving from the nature of things" (3).
[31] "It is better to say that the government most in conformity with nature is the one whose particular arrangement best relates to the disposition of the people for whom it is established" (8).
[32] "Individual strengths cannot be united unless all wills are united" (8).

Montesquieu is concerned with social phenomena rather than with the mind of the individual (17).

Montesquieu's story of the Troglodytes in *Lettres persanes* presents an argument about society and law in an allegorical format. As he had done in *Esprit des lois*, Montesquieu sought to dispute Hobbes' theory that human beings are evil by nature. The allegory demonstrates that, as Shackleton observes, "Hobbes is indeed wrong, since a community inspired entirely by the self-interest of its individual members perishes" (38). The first Troglodyte society described by Montesquieu dispensed with formal political organization and each person followed his or her own self-centered instincts. This society disintegrated, however, but two families survived. Montesquieu blames the downfall of this evil and unjust society on each individual's selfishness: "Tous les particuliers convinrent qu'ils n'obéiraient plus à personne; que chacun veillerait uniquement à ses intérêts, sans consulter ceux des autres" (68).[33] Out of this self-destructive society, a new society was formed by the two remaining families who built a new society based on virtue and a newly chosen king to govern them. Rather than being guided by selfish ambition, each individual chose to concentrate on the interest of others, and to instruct others to be virtuous as well:

> Ils travaillaient avec une sollicitude commune pour l'intérêt commun
> . . . Toute leur attention était d'élever leurs enfants à la vertu . . . Ils
> leur faisaient surtout sentir que l'intérêt des particuliers se trouve
> toujours dans l'intérêt commun. (69)[34]

The differences between the two Troglodyte societies can be attributed to a dual human nature. Merry argues that Montesquieu's fable reveals two different and opposing sides to human nature. Individuals are naturally just and virtuous, and are

---

[33] "All of them agreed that they would no longer obey anyone at all; each was to attend only to his personal interests, and to consider none other" (23).

[34] "They labored together for their mutual benefit . . . . Their entire attention was directed to educating their children in the ways of virtue . . . . They were taught that individual interest is always bound to the common interest" (26).

inclined towards the common interest; but at the same time, their nature allows them to be competitive and selfish as well (Merry 11). Individuals are thus neither entirely evil by nature nor are they entirely virtuous. Societies need the restraining rule of law to hold individuals' competitive side in check. A society based on virtue needs the rule of reasonable laws as well, as individuals will find it difficult to live under their own restraint (Merry 11).

Helvétius identifies the role of societies and of their legislation as one which forces individuals to restrain or govern their passions – the consequence of transformed physical sensations – in such a way as to make them conform to the interests of the society. His considerations of the establishment of law and of virtue in society stress the role of the individual's self-interest. Human behavior is explained by self-interest, reducible to physical need (Martin 5) and as individuals experience physical pain, pleasure, or need, they develop a desire to fulfill those needs, increase their pleasure, or decrease their pain. The physical sensations cause the individuals to form a self-interest, or "amour de soi" (125), and this personal interest leads to the individuals' urge to assemble with others in order to satisfy their own needs better. Society is thus born out of self-interest. Helvétius traces the development of society by beginning with the moment in time that preceded any knowledge of laws, "aux premiers jours du monde" (129). At that time, individuals were scattered in the woods and were unable, without the help of others, to fend off animal attacks. Because of their fear or sense of danger, they discovered that it was in their own self-interest to form a union with others in order to ward off a common enemy. This "ligue contre les animaux" was Helvétius' conception of the first society (130). What follows this initial phase of society is war and conflict. Unlike Hobbes who saw war as the initial stage of human existence, Helvétius considers it an outgrowth of the social contact between individuals. Societies cannot survive this state of war, however, without the creation of new agreements, whereby individuals renounce their self-interest and mutually work towards the preservation of life of all members of the society. By establishing this new pact, individuals act in harmony with a common interest, and acquire ideas of justice and injustice, based on what is useful or injurious to society (130). Moreover, through the respect of "conventions," humans acquire the notion of virtue. The individual in nature, not having entered into conventions with others, obeys only passions, whereas individuals in society acquire virtue by sacrificing their own interest to that of the public interest. Helvétius describes this connection between the individual's sensitivity and society in the following manner:

> Sans la sensiblité à la douleur et au plaisir physique, les hommes, sans désirs, sans passions, également indifférents à tous, n'eussent point connu d'intérêt personnel; que sans intérêt personnel ils ne se fussent point rassemblés en société, n'eussent point fait entre eux de conventions; qu'il n'y eût point eu d'intérêt général, par conséquent point d'actions justes ou injustes; et qu'ainsi la sensibilité physique et l'intérêt personnel ont été les auteurs de toute justice. (130-31)[35]

The mechanisms of organized society therefore direct its members away from self-interest and towards the general interest in order to make them become virtuous. Moral value, virtues and vices exist only in the context of society and the self-interest of its participants.

Laws and legislation are legitimate within this context because they codify what is useful to society – virtue – and what is harmful – vice. Laws exist to ensure that human beings are just. According to Helvétius, "C'est donc uniquement par de bonnes lois qu'on peut former des hommes vertueux" (124).[36] The duty of the legislator, then, is to create laws that clearly spell out how individuals are to conform their interest to the general interest: "Tout l'art du législateur consiste donc à forcer les hommes, par le sentiment de l'amour d'eux-mêmes, d'être toujours justes les uns

---

[35] " . . . without a sensibility of pain and natural pleasure, men, without desires, without passions, and equally indifferent with respect to every thing, would not have known a personal interest: that without personal interest they would not have united in society, would not have entered into conventions amongst themselves, and would not have had a general interest; consequently there would have been no actions, either just or unjust; and that thus natural sensibility and personal interest have been the authors of all justice" (213).

[36] "It is then only by good laws that we can form virtuous men" (184).

envers les autres" (124).[37] The general interest, now that Helvétius has established
it within the context of legislators and legislation, can be considered as synonymous
with the interest of the state; consequently, by serving the general interest, the
individual serves the interest of the state. Or as Foucault suggests, the legislator must
be concerned with how an individual will best be used to further the goals of the
state. O'Neal refers to this as Helvétius' "utilitarianism" where private interests
happily coexist with the public interest, thus constituting virtue (92). D'Holbach also
referred to the utility of individuals in society in his assertion that because humans
are neither good nor evil by nature, they must be informed of what is good and evil
once they enter into society. His concept of this societal dictate of vice and virtue is
based on the happiness of the community, an idea similarly put forth by Helvétius.
In *Système social* he explains that happiness is in fact the basis of the social pact. As
all individuals search to secure their own happiness, they are able to do so only with
the help of others.

> Si tout homme tend au bonheur, toute société se propose le même
> but; & c'est pour être heureux que l'homme vit en société. Ainsi, la
> Société est un assemblage d'hommes, réunis par leurs besoins, pour
> travailler de concert à leur conservation & à leur félicité commune.
> (*SS* II: 4)[38]

This reciprocal relationship between the individual and society requires each
individual to work towards the happiness of all. What is useful to society's
happiness defines virtue, and what is harmful to society's happiness is vice. The
individual's worth is thus based on his or her utility to the common good: "Un
homme est bon, raisonnable, vertueux ... lorsque ses passions sont utiles à lui-même

---

[37] "All the art therefore of the legislator consists in forcing them by self-love to be always just to each other" (185).
[38] "If every man is inclined towards happiness, all societies offer this same goal. Man lives in society to be happy. Therefore, society is an assembly of men, united according their needs in order to work in concert towards their preservation and common happiness."

& aux êtres avec lesquels il se trouve associé" (*SS* I: 11).[39] It is the government's duty, therefore, to direct the passions of their society towards the good of all.

According to Diderot, in the state of pure nature, individuals were primarily focused on the self, and, as Helvétius had also imagined, were motivated by fear. Individuals developed, nevertheless, a relationship with others as humans lived in loosely organized communities like those of the animals. This development demonstrates for Diderot the human realization that individual interests are best served by a conjunction of interests. Diderot points out in *Observations sur le Nakaz* that society developed because, "c'est la nécessité de lutter contre l'ennemi commun . . . qui a rassemblé les hommes. Ils ont senti qu'ils luttaient plus avantageusement avec des forces réunies qu'avec des forces séparées" (402).[40] Individuals thus formed societies by mutual consent coupled with an instinct to congregate: "Les hommes se sont réunis en société par instinct" (*Observations* 403).[41]

As the individuals come together to form a society, they also communally agree to be subject to an authority which will serve the common interest. Diderot's article for the *Encyclopédie*, "Autorité politique," analyzes the concept of authority in-depth. Political authority is not natural, he explains, except, perhaps, for paternal authority over the family:

> Aucun homme n'a reçu de la nature le droit de commander aux autres. . . . Si la nature a établi quelque *autorité,* c'est la puissance paternelle: mais la puissance paternelle a ses bornes; & dans l'état de nature elle finirait aussitôt que les enfants seraient en état de se conduire. Toute autre *autorité* vient d'une autre origine que de la nature. (537)[42]

---

[39] "A man is good, reasonable, virtuous . . . when his passions are useful to himself and to the others with whom he is associated."

[40] "It was the necessity of struggling against the ever-present, common enemy – nature – which brought men together. They became aware that they struggled to better effect together, than separately" (*PW* 124.

[41] "Men gathered together in society by instinct" (*PW* 124).

[42] "No man has by nature been granted the right to command others. . . . If nature has established any authority, it is that of paternal power; but paternal power has its limits, and in the state of nature it would end as soon as children were able to look after themselves. All other authority originates

The prince to whom the society subjects itself is limited, however, by the laws of nature and of the state, and is also in fact bound to the people he governs. "Le prince tient de ses sujets mêmes *l'autorité* qu'il a sur eux; & cette autorité est bornée par les lois de la nature & de l'état" (Autorité 539).[43] These laws are the conditions under which the people submitted to authority: by their own choice and consent. This theory is defined as the social compact, whereby the individuals in the society are bound to their prince and vice versa (Mason and Wokler xii).

Within society, justice and injustice are expressed through a *volonté générale*, or general will. Diderot's notion of the general will reveals his belief that the self-interest of individuals in the *état de troupeau* translates into an agreement to combine the private interests with those of the whole (Mason and Wokler xiii). Diderot writes in, "Droit naturel," that it is the submission to a general will that ties societies together. He employs the term "*volonté générale*," which will become a key ingredient in Rousseau's *Du contrat social*, to express the way in which all individuals participate collectively, through the natural reasoning of which all humans are capable, to determine the natural rights of humanity. Diderot writes, "La volonté générale est dans chaque individu un acte pur de l'entendement qui raisonne dans le silence des passions sur ce que l'homme peut exiger de son semblable, & sur ce que son semblable est en droit d'exiger de lui" (Droit 28).[44] Rather than entrusting one individual with the determination of natural rights, the issue is left to all members of the human race as they partake of the general will (Mason and Wokler xiii). The individual is brought into conformity with the general will and must refer to it: "C'est à la volonté générale que l'individu doit s'adresser pour savoir jusqu'où

---

outside of nature" (*PW* 6).

[43] "It is from his subjects that the prince derives the authority that he exercises over them, and this authority is limited by the laws of nature and of the state" (*PW* 8).

[44] "The general will is in each person a pure expression of the understanding, which in the silence of passions calculates what every individual may demand from his fellow-man and what his fellow-man has a right to demand of him" (*PW* 21).

il doit être homme, citoyen, sujet, père, enfant" (Droit 28).[45] Furthermore, he reiterates throughout his article that this general will is always correct. Contrary to the will of one individual, which can be mistaken, the general will is never wrong regarding the good of humanity and the nature of right and wrong. Diderot explains this as follows:

> Mais si nous ôtons à l'individu le droit de décider de la nature du juste & de l'injuste, où porterons-nous cette grande question? où? devant le genre humain: c'est à lui seul qu'il appartient de la décider parce que le bien de tous est la seule passion qu'il ait. Les volontés particulières sont suspectes; elles peuvent être bonnes ou méchantes, mais la volonté générale est toujours bonne: elle n'a jamais trompé, elle ne trompera jamais. (Droit 27)[46]

In Diderot's analysis, the individual's personal interest can thus be held in check by referring to the general will of humanity.

As individuals conform to the general will, they do not, however, lose their identity as individuals. Each individual differs physically from others, particularly in the way in which the brain processes information and causes a reaction (J. Perkins 122). J. Perkins has pointed out that after 1772, upon considering Helvétius' *De l'homme*, Diderot began to examine more closely the individual human being (121). Helvétius had concluded that all individuals were made up of the same organized matter, and differed only as a result of external influences. Diderot, however, seems to refute this conclusion in his commentary on François Hemsterhuis' *Lettre sur l'homme et ses rapports*. Hemsterhuis reflects on human knowledge, proposing that in primitive society all individuals were equal in intelligence and sensations (336). Diderot responds to this proposition by noting that in such a society, "il n'y aurait

---

[45] "For an individual to know how far he ought to be a man, a citizen, a subject, a father, or a child . . . he must address himself to the general will" (*PW* 20).

[46] "But if we deny the individual the right to determine the nature of justice and injustice, before which bar shall we plead this great question? Where? Before mankind. Mankind alone must settle the matter, because it has no other craving than the good of all. Private wills are suspect; they may be either good or bad. But the general will is always good" (*PW* 19).

plus de *moi,* il n'y aurait qu'un être; l'individu ne tarderait pas à s'identifier avec tous les autres" (Hemsterhuis 337).[47]

Similar to Diderot, but certainly a much lesser-known *philosophe,* Morelly had based his ideas of law on his conception of human nature, emphasizing the human inclination towards sociability.[48] The individual as defined by Morelly is a necessary part of a whole, or as he notes in a work called *Le Prince,* each individual exists to serve as "la partie *complétive* d'un *Tout*" (2). Individuals are by nature sociable and are born in a state of mutual dependence (*Code* 220). This natural sociability is explained by the individual's inability to provide for one's self and the implicit admission that the help of others is needed to fulfill one's physical needs. He explains this in *Code de la nature,*

> [La Nature] a voulu que la peine, la fatigue de pourvoir à nos besoins, toujours un peu plus étendus que nos forces, quand nous sommes seuls, nous fit comprendre la nécessité de recourir à des secours . . . ; delà notre aversion pour l'abandon et la solitude, notre amour pour les agrémens et les avantages d'une puissante réunion, d'une *société.* (169)[49]

He goes on to say that the sentiment of sociability was corrupted as societies grew, loosened the bonds between families, transmigrated, and finally, established the notion of private property. Often described as a precursor to communism, Morelly points specifically to private property as the source of evil self-interest and the discord of individual wills (Driver 223). Private property must therefore be abolished according to his program of reform intended to ensure a return to a natural state of sociability and virtue.

---

[47] "There would no longer be an *I*; there would only be one being; the individual would not delay in identifying with others."

[48] In fact, some nineteenth-century writers confused Morelly's writings with Diderot's, and attributed Morelly's *Code de la nature,* published in 1755, to Diderot (Driver 218).

[49] "Nature wished that when we are isolated, the pain and the fatigue of providing for our needs, which are always greater than our strength, make us understand the necessity of seeking help . . . ; thus our aversion for abandonment and solitude, our love for approval and the advantages of a powerful union, of a society."

His ideal legislation, outlined in the final chapter of his *Code,* is one that conforms to the laws and intentions of nature, wherein individuals serve the society rather than themselves. The first several laws listed as his "loix fondamentales et sacrées" are in fact related to the denial of the individual's private property and private lives. In the first of these, he dictates that, "Rien dans la Société n'appartiendra singulièrement ni en propriété à personne" (286).[50] This law is followed by others that identify the individual as a public servant to be supported and maintained by society, and who in turn must contribute to the public utility.[51] In the laws that follow, he carefully prescribes roles and duties for each individual, noting the division of labor, service to governmental bodies, education, and, among other things, marriage practices. His vision for a perfect society is clearly one that singles out individuals in an order designed to fulfill the purposes of the state.

Rousseau's conceptualization of the individual

Rousseau's conceptualization of the individual human being is inextricably linked with his view of nature. Durkheim stressed the importance of the individual in Rousseau's analysis of the origin of societies. In Rousseau's state of nature, the notion of the individual is of primary concern. "There is nothing beyond the individual," Durkheim writes (85). The individual is conceived of as the foundation of society:

> [Rousseau] starts with the individual and, without ascribing to him the slightest social inclination or conflicting tendencies suah as might tend, through the evils to which they rise, to make society necessary, he undertakes to explain how a being so fundamentally indifferent to any kind of life in common came to form societies. (80)

---

[50] "No one in society has sole ownership of anything."
[51] "Tout Citoyen sera homme public sustenté, entretenu et occupé aux dépens du Public;" "Tout Citoyen contribuera pour sa part à l'utilité publique" (286).

Rousseau's point of departure for much of his theorizing about and understanding of humanity is a hypothetical state of nature which served to guide his investigation. In the preface to the *Discours sur l'inégalité,* he describes the state of nature as a "un état qui n'existe plus, qui n'a peut-être point existé, qui probablement n'existera jamais" (159).[52] His purpose is to define the "probable" evolution of humanity, and he acknowledges here that his theory of the development of humanity is strictly hypothetical (Launay 207-8). Rousseau's state of nature was not a pre-social historical period, but was intended to suggest what man would be "without what he owes to society, reduced to what he would be if he had always lived in isolation" (Durkheim 66). This concept of nature as a pre-social state is certainly not original, because classical thought, particularly in the works of the natural law philosophers, speculated on a hypothetical state of nature in order to determine the origins of society and a social contract (Bloch and Bloch 26). Yet in Rousseau's analysis, the state of nature is not only posited in contrast to society in a chronological sense – i.e. not occurring simultaneously – he also opposes the state of nature to the corruption of society. His interpretation of the creation of society is a negative one, thus placing his ideas in contradiction to the convictions of such thinkers as Buffon and Diderot, who saw society as the natural milieu where humans found conditions for their survival and progress (Duchet 332). Society was by contrast the milieu that made its members selfish, depraved, and subservient, as he suggests in his *Discours sur les sciences et les arts* and elsewhere.

Individuals lived in isolation from one another, not because they had an aversion to others but because they had no natural need for them. By refusing to attribute to the natural state an original social instinct to guide individuals towards society, Rousseau found himself in disagreement with natural law philosophers (Cassirer 259). Humans were not dependent on others to meet their physical needs, he asserted, but were entirely self-sufficient, seeking their own self-preservation

---

[52] " . . . a state which no longer exists, perhaps never did exist, and probably never will exist"(44).

without any recourse to others. "Le premier sentiment de l'homme fut celui de son
existence, son premier soin celui de sa conservation" (*Inégalité* 222).[53] Rousseau
explains that in the pure state of nature,

> errant dans les forêts sans industrie, sans parole, sans domicile, sans
> guerre, et sans liaisons, sans nul besoin de ses semblables, comme
> sans nul désir de leur nuire, peut-être même sans jamais en
> reconnaître aucun individuellement, l'homme sauvage sujet à peu de
> passions, et se suffisant à lui-même, n'avait que les sentiments et les
> lumières propres à cet état. (*Inégalité* 218)[54]

The individual in nature – self-reliant, self-centered – does not merely avoid conflict
or relationships with others, but is completely indifferent towards them, and even
then, seem incapable of recognizing their presence. This isolated individual's only
reality is the realm of the self, or is solipsistic (J. Perkins 92-93).

Isolated individuals eventually form ties with one another nevertheless, but
not because of a natural inclination towards society; rather, it is because of external
circumstances that create new needs. Mutual assistance was not naturally necessary
since, according to Rousseau, each individual is capable of self-sufficiency.
Consequently in order for a society to be formed, external circumstances had to
change one's physical needs and to modify one's nature (Durkheim 81). In *Du
contrat social* as well as in his *Essai sur l'origine des langues* Rousseau describes
how these obstacles arise, against which the individual cannot combat, changing the
physical needs of isolated individuals. He writes,

> Je suppose les hommes parvenus à ce point où les obstacles qui
> nuisent à leur conservation dans l'état de nature l'emportent par leur
> résistance sur les forces que chaque individu peut employer pour se
> maintenir dans cet état. Alors cet état primitif ne peut plus subsister,

---

[53] "Man's first feeling was that of his own existence, and his first care that of self-preservation" (84).
[54] " . . . wandering up and down the forests, without industry, without speech, and without home, an
equal stranger to war and to all ties, neither standing in need of his fellow-creatures nor having any
desire to hurt them, and perhaps even not distinguishing them one from another; let us conclude that,
being self-sufficient and subject to so few passions, he could have no feelings or knowledge but such
as befitted his situation" (79).

et le genre humain périrait s'il ne changerait sa manière d'être. (*Contrat* 38)[55]

Rousseau clarifies in his *Essai sur l'origine des langues* that these "obstacles" to self-preservation are in fact related to climatic influences and the physical environment. In climates that are warm and hospitable to human life, societies formed much more slowly because humans could more easily survive without one another (*Essai* 388). On the other hand, in colder climates, self-preservation was much more difficult and, therefore, isolated individuals saw the benefit of cooperating with others in order to survive: "Il falloit songer à vivre. Le besoin mutuel unissant les hommes bien mieux que le sentiment n'auroit fait, la société ne se forma que par l'industrie" (*Essai* 394).[56] This realization of the need for cooperation in a harsh physical environment gave rise to language, where the first words uttered were a call for others: the words, "aidez-moi" (*Essai* 394). In his discourse on inequality, Rousseau emphasized the link between the development of society, the creation of private property, and of course, the introduction of inequality, and he noted here, too, that this process was set in motion "dès l'instant qu'un homme eut besoin du secours d'un autre" (*Inégalité* 232).[57] Society is therefore a creation – an artificial entity because there is no natural impulse towards it.

Rousseau's treatise on education, *Emile*, presents a hypothetical individual, Emile, whose experiences are controlled by a tutor who seeks to establish the ideal – most natural – education in order to prepare him for a moral life in an immoral, corrupted society. The individual Emile is theorized not within a pre-social state, as in the discourses, but outside the social context and within a context that isolates him

---

[55] "I make the assumption that there is a point in the development of mankind at which the obstacles to men's self-preservation in the state of nature are too great to be overcome by the strength that any one individual can exert in order to maintain himself in this state. The original state can then subsist no longer and the human race would perish if it did not change its mode of existence" (54). [The bibliography includes two entries for an English translation of *Contrat social*; the Oxford edition is the one that is used in this chapter.]

[56] " . . . one had to be concerned with living. Mutual need uniting men to greater extent when sentiment has not done so, society would be formed only through industry" (48).

[57] " . . . from the moment when man began to stand in need of the help of another" (92).

from the contamination by society (Crocker 134). Nature is here presented differently from the pre-social state described in Rousseau's discourses or *Essai sur l'origine des langues.* Although Emile becomes more individualized and concrete throughout the course of the novel (J. Perkins 94), *Emile* is nevertheless the study of an *abstract individual* who has no innate ideas but who is formed and molded by his tutor in such a way as to reflect nature's intentions. The individual is theorized not within a pre-social state, but outside the social context, not belonging to a "prehistorical past" but to a "hypothetical future" (Crocker 133-34).

Emile serves to bridge the gap between Rousseau's discourses, *Essai sur l'origine des langues,* and his more overtly political works, *Economie politique* and the *Du contrat social.* Crocker explains this connection: "[*Emile* and *Du contrat social*] are steps towards Rousseau's grand plan for the good society. . . . these works are political, in the large sense of that word. Their subject is how to govern men" (133). Crocker's interpretation of Emile as a "reconstructed individual" who is subject to "behavioral engineering" by the tutor sheds light on our understanding of Rousseau's notion of the individual. Rousseau's individual in *Emile* is not an abstraction of a human being, but one who can be manipulated, or reconstructed as Crocker characterizes it, if the education is done properly. An important element in this education, however, is the care taken to prevent Emile from realizing the very fact that he is being controlled. Rousseau writes of the pupil, "Qu'il croie toujours être le maître, et que ce soit toujours vous qui le soyez. Il n'y a point d'assujettissement si parfait que celui qui garde l'apparence de la liberté" (114).[58] Emile is led to believe in a lie: that he is in control of his experiences and learning when in fact he has no control over them whatsoever. In a paradoxical way, Rousseau exalts the individual Emile but at the same time he disallows him from having an authentic individuality. This individual found in *Emile* is, however, a basis

---

[58] "Let him always fancy that he is the master, but let it always be yourself that really governs. There is no subjugation so perfect as that which preserves the appearance of liberty" (87).

for the concrete individuals that make up society as described in *Economie politique,* an article he wrote for the *Encyclopédie.*

An effective government, Rousseau suggests in *Economie politique,* must adequately control the members of that community. Previously, according to Rousseau, *économie* referred to the governing of the home for the benefit of the "bien commun" of the family (*Economie* 240). But, he wrote, this meaning is no longer valid, because the term has come to encompass the government of "la grande famille, qui est l'état" (*Economie* 240). The issue of political economy as expressed by Rousseau is addressed by Foucault in his discussion on governmentality. He summarizes Rousseau's conclusions by saying that in order to govern a state well, "economy" must be applied, where the government must *surveiller* and control the inhabitants in the same way in which the head of a household manages a family. Foucault notes,

> To govern a state will therefore mean to apply economy . . . which means exercising towards its inhabitants, and the wealth and behaviour of each and all, a form of surveillance and control as attentive as that of the head of a family over his household and his goods. (Governmentality 92)

This management requires education and control of each individual in the community, Rousseau points out, "Ce n'est pas assez de dire aux citoyens, soyez bons; il faut leur *apprendre* à l'être" (emphasis added; *Economie* 254).[59] In other words, the society needs "Emiles" who can be taught and molded by a government who serves as the tutor. "S'il est bon de savoir employer les hommes tels qu'ils sont, il vaut beaucoup mieux encore les rendre tels qu'on a besoin qu'ils soient," writes Rousseau (*Economie* 251).[60] Theorizing in *Emile,* Rousseau attempts to carry out his

---

[59] "It is not enough to say to the citizens, be good; they must be taught to be so" (142). [The bibliography includes two entries for an English translation of *Economie politique;* the Knopf edition is the one that is used here.]
[60] "If it is good to know how to deal with men as they are, it is much better to make them what there is need that they should be" (139).

ideas in practice in *Economie politique*. Here, the reconstructed individual is of utmost concern for the good of the state and exists to fulfill the purposes of the state. Rousseau's concept of the "well-ordered society" demands that each individual be directed towards the whole of the community, and vice versa (Viroli 40).

Discussing the concept of the general will in *Economie politique*, Rousseau writes that one of the essential rules of legitimate government is to be sure that the general will is accomplished by making all individual wills conform: "*Faites* que toutes les volontés particulières s'y rapportent" (emphasis added; *Economie* 252).[61] And in doing so, a new morality is born. In nature, there was no morality; humans were neither moral nor immoral, whereas in the civil state, morality is derived from the requirement that individuals follow a general will. In *Du contrat social*, Rousseau explains that the transition from a state of nature to the civil state "produit dans l'homme un changement remarquable, en . . . donnant à ses actions la moralité qui leur manquait auparavant" (43).[62] This morality, or virtue, is explained in *Economie politique* as having a sharply political meaning: "La vertu n'est que cette conformité de la volonté particulière à la générale" (252).[63] Since virtue is not natural, it is artificial and must be created and formed; individuals must learn how to be virtuous. It is the role of the legislator – similar to that of the tutor of *Emile* – to guide them to be so. Rousseau justifies the legislator thusly: "Tous ont également besoin de guides. Il faut obliger les uns à conformer leurs volontés à leur raison; il faut apprendre à l'autre à connaître ce qu'il veut" (*Contrat* 64).[64]

In *Julie*, Rousseau provides a microcosm for the society he discusses in *Economie politique* and *Du contrat social*. Clarens is described as Rousseau's ideal society, where Wolmar's role is similar to that of the legislator of the *Du contrat*

---

[61] "Bring all the particular will into conformity with it" (140).
[62] " . . . produces in a man a very remarkable change, and ... conferring on his actions the moral quality that they had lacked before" (59).
[63] "Virtue is nothing more than this conformity of the particular wills with the general will" (140).
[64] "All equally need guides. The one side must be obliged to shape their wills to their reason, the other must be taught the knowledge of what it wants" (75).

social. Each individual is guided by the superior intelligence of the legislator, so that the individual, while believing to be free to reason is actually bringing the private will into accordance with the reasonable, general one[65]: "Tout l'art du maître est de cacher cette gêne sous le voile du plaisir et de l'intérêt, en sorte qu'ils pensent vouloir tout ce qu'on les oblige à faire" (*Julie* 339).[66] This idea is similarly expressed in the *Contrat social* where Rousseau famously phrased it, "Quiconque refusera d'obéir à la volonté générale y sera constraint par tout le corps: ce qui ne signifie autre chose sinon qu'on le forcera d'être libre" (*Contrat* 43).[67]

Rousseau's system for the organization of society as described in *Du contrat social* provides a way for individuals to be virtuous, happy, and free while at the same time live in the unnatural condition of interdependence. The *Contrat social* explains that once the state of nature is no longer sustainable, "le genre humain périrait s'il ne changeait sa manière d'être" (38).[68] Thus the isolated individual in the primitive state must be transformed in order to have an acceptable environment in which to live. This new state is one which is reconstructed as Crocker describes it. There is a strong connection between the reconstructed individual in *Emile* and the reconstructed society in *Du contrat social*: "The reconstructed society cannot be realized without postulating the reconstructed individual, and the latter cannot be realized without the former" (Crocker 173). Rousseau does not suggest a return to the primitive state of pure nature. Instead, he searches for a constituted societal system whereby individuals are politically united for mutual protection but maintain their personal liberty rather than being subject to the tyranny of society. The goal of *Du contrat social* is summed up as follows:

---

[65] Duchet makes this point in *Anthropologie et histoire* (362-368), bringing Wolmar's comment to my attention.
[66] "The master's whole art consists in hiding this coercion under the veil of pleasure or interest, so that they think they desire all they are obliged to do" (373).
[67] "If anyone refuses to obey the general will he will be compelled to do so by the whole body; which means nothing else than that he will be forced to be free" (58).
[68] "The human race would perish if it did not change its mode of existence" (54).

> Trouver une forme d'association qui défende et protège de toute la
> force commune la personne et les biens de chaque associé, et par
> laquelle chacun s'unissant à tous n'obéisse pourtant qu'à lui-même
> et reste aussi libre qu'auparavant. (39)[69]

This form of association does not call for an abdication of one's liberty, but a transformation of the independent self into the aggregate of individuals that compose society. This requires the termination of natural independence and solitude. It is necessary to "transformer chaque individu, qui par lui-même est un tout parfait et solitaire, en partie d'un plus grand tout dont cet individu reçoive en quelque sorte sa vie et son être" (*Contrat* 65).[70] The individual's identity is thus strictly linked to the association with the society.

Rousseau believes that each particular will ceases to function as such, and blends into the composition of the general will and is expressed through it. In submitting to the general will, the individual is not subjugated to any other particular will: "Chacun se donnant à tous ne se donne à personne" (*Contrat* 39).[71] The general will that emerges is superior to any individual will, and consequently, all individuals have placed their "personne" and "puissance" under "la suprême direction de la volonté générale" (*Contrat* 40).[72] Cassirer explains that in Rousseau's system, when individuals renounce the independence they had in nature and engage in the social contract, "they have become individuals in the higher sense: they have become subjects governed by the will whereas heretofore they had been motivated by their appetites and sense passions" (261). In Rousseau's reconstructed society, the individuals must be weaned away from nature and deprived of their independent existence, so that each individual becomes part of a communal self (Viroli 42-43).

---

[69] "Find a form of association which will defend and protect, with the whole of its joint strength, the person and property of each associate, and under which each of them, uniting himself to all, will obey himself alone and remain as free as before" (54).

[70] " . . . transforming each individual, who in himself is a perfect, isolated whole, into a part of a larger whole from which the individual, as it were, receives his life and being" (76).

[71] "Each in giving himself to all gives himself to none" (55).

[72] Their "person" and their "power" under "the supreme direction of the general will."

Rousseau calls this communal self, "son *moi* commun," where the ensemble of each contracting individual forms a collective but single and unified body (*Contrat* 40). Rousseau compares the functioning of the political body to that of the human body. In *Economie politique* he compares the human body's members to the citizens of a state. He thus reveals the importance of all parts as they contribute to the movement of the whole body; each part is not distinct and capable of independent activity. The body, like the general will, does not consist of a mere arithmetical sum of individual organs, but of a singular, unified entity. The sum of individuals form the society, but the creation of society is not natural to the individuals. At the same time, the individual identity becomes lost within the context of the general will.

The notion of the individual therefore undergoes a transformation from Rousseau's ideas on the state of nature to his theories of society. In nature the individual is conceived of as an abstract, but independent pre-social being, but once society has been established, the individual gains consideration as a concrete being. In nature, individuals are primarily concerned with their self-preservation and are not inclined towards the happiness of others. Therefore, to have a happy and virtuous society, this nature must be suppressed by denying the individual of an identity that is contrary to the general will. An individual will that does not become fused with the general will is aberrant and acts as a barrier to the general will, which Bates calls "errant individuality" (76-77). If the sovereign authority of a state exists within the general will, not within a sum of particular wills, there can be no private wills without causing social disorder. Durkheim expresses the individual's potential menace to the social order:

> The social objective must be stripped of all individual character. . . .
> It is necessary to submerge him in the mass, in order to modify his
> nature as much as possible and prevent him from acting as an
> individual. Anything of a nature to facilitate individual action must
> be regarded as a danger. (108)

Concluding remarks

The eighteenth-century *philosophes'* attempts to define the individual human being relied on their careful reasoning and abstract understanding of the place human beings occupy in the universe. Indeed, as Foucault points out, they were able to speak of the human mind and of the body and of human being's place in the world. The conceptual framework established by the *philosophes,* however, proved inadequate and insufficient when the revolutionaries attempted to establish a new political and societal system for France. The revolutionaries' concept of sovereignty was based on the theory of the general will, which required a cohesion of individual wills. Whether the individual human was a strictly material being, or was subject to the laws of movement or to physical sensations was ultimately of little consequence. Practical concerns of legitimizing the new political power outweighed abstract reasoning about human nature. The revolutionaries were thus forced to confront new ways of viewing the concrete individuals that composed the foundation for the newly established form of popular sovereignty.

Chapter Three

The French Revolution's Struggle to Reconcile
the Abstract Individual and the Concrete Individual

Le peuple vaut toujours mieux que les individus.
Robespierre

Addressing the National Convention on February 5, 1794, Robespierre declared that among his visions for France was, "un ordre de choses . . . où la Patrie assure le bien-être de chaque individu, et où chaque individu jouisse avec orgueil de la prospérité et de la gloire de la Patrie" (10: 352).[1] Stating this goal at the height of the revolution and only months before his own execution, he stressed the Revolution's ideals of liberty and happiness for each individual citizen, and at the same time, subtly revealed the difficulty in accomplishing such a goal. By this time, almost five years had passed since the storming of the Bastille, yet many of the Revolution's goals remained elusive. The celebration of the individual's liberty was still a characteristic of revolutionary rhetoric, but the notion of the individual had undergone a transformation that belied this celebration.

The individual will versus the general will

The notion of the individual presents countless contradictions and ambiguities in revolutionary discourse and ideology. While the *philosophes* based their

---

[1] " . . . an order of things . . . where our country assures the well-being of each individual, and where each individual proudly enjoys our country's prosperity and glory" (370). This quotation is taken from the volume of revolutionary documents edited by Keith Michael Baker, *The Old Regime and the French Revolution*. All subsequent quotations from this source will be abbreviated *ORFR*.

understanding of the individual's role in society on their understanding of nature, the Revolution's thinkers based their understanding on the theory and practice of political principles. The principles that guided revolutionary thought are familiar: liberty, equality, virtue, and popular sovereignty. It was according to these precepts, and their fierce devotion to them, that the Revolution's leaders, particularly the Jacobins, developed their views concerning the individual in revolutionary society. Central to their understanding of them was the notion of a unified, indivisible citizenry according to which each individual joins in the cohesion that creates the unanimous body politic and general will. The fusion of individuals was a fundamental consequence of the basic tenets of popular sovereignty; it also implied that each individual was likewise critical to the proper functioning of the state. When the individual sought to assert a personal interest, however, he or she was a source of dissention and posed a threat to unity. As a result, the individual was viewed with suspicion. Hence, the contradictory relationship between the individual and the body politic. Jaume succinctly describes this conflict: "L'individu joue à la fois le rôle d'une entité indispensable et d'une source d'intérêt particulier, comme telle frappée de soupçon" (216).[2] Popular sovereignty could become legitimate only through a coalescence of wills and could not survive with a predominance of private interests.

The assertion of popular sovereignty, according to which sovereignty resides within each rights-bearing individual, forced the identity and definition of the individual to come to the fore. If the sovereign authority of the state ultimately dwells within each individual, then the individual – the basic political unit – must surrender personal interest to the collective interest embodied in the general will. In so doing, each individual citizen no longer lays claim to an independent will, but contributes to the collective will of the sovereign body. The individual will is therefore the fundamental element of the general will, and likewise, the individual

---

[2] "The individual simultaneously plays the role of an indispensable entity and a source of individual interest, and as such is marked with suspicion."

is the fundamental element of the political body. Rousseau explains this reciprocal relationship between the individual and the collective body in the sovereign society:

> L'acte d'association renferme un engagement réciproque du public avec les particuliers, et que chaque individu, contractant, pour ainsi dire, avec lui-même, se trouve engagé sous un double rapport; savoir, comme membre du souverain envers les particuliers, et comme membre de l'Etat envers le souverain. (*Contrat* 41)[3]

It is the participation of each individual in this dual-role process of partaking in sovereignty and being subject to it that causes the individual to become a focal point of sovereign society and simultaneously to disappear as a solitary, independent will.

This abstract process provided the theoretical foundation for the profound changes that began in 1789. The new type of sovereignty, and therefore the success of the Revolution, was dependent on the willingness of each member of society to accept his or her role as a contributor to the general will. In his 1789 pamphlet that defined the goals of the Third Estate, *Qu'est-ce que le tiers état?*, Abbé Sieyès stated in simple terms that, "les volontés individuelles sont les seuls élémens de la volonté commune" (189).[4] If the basic unit of the general will is the individual will, then each individual will is an essential building block of the body politic. During the revolutionary period, the individual was valorized in two ways. First of all, the individual was considered in an abstract manner, as an intangible will or interest that combined with others to form an association. Secondly, the individual was also a material human being whose speech and actions were expressions of that will. The revolutionaries were therefore forced to struggle with both of these aspects of the individual: the abstract individual as well as the concrete individual. Reconciling the two would prove to be at the crux of the Revolution's increasingly radical direction.

---

[3] "The act of association comprises a mutual undertaking between the public and the individuals, and that each individual, in making a contract, as we may say, with himself, is bound in a double reaction; as a member of the Sovereign he is bound to the individuals, and as a member of the State to the Sovereign" (192). [The bibliography includes two entries for an English translation of *Contrat social*; the Knopf edition is the one that is used in this chapter.]

[4] "The sole elements of the common will are individual wills" (*ORFR* 175).

Each individual citizen was now of utmost concern for the state. Foucault notes this development and observes that the modern political state's power was in fact characterized by the increasing concern with individuals. He writes that the form of state power that began to appear in the sixteenth century and proceeded through the eighteenth century, was both an "individualizing and totalizing form of power" (Subject 213). The individualizing form of power, as Graham Burchell has explained, is a characteristic of a government that is "concerned with concrete lives and conduct of individuals" (121). The Revolution clearly manifested this form of power and the revolutionary government was indeed preoccupied with the speech and actions of individuals. Citizens became individualized because their lives and conduct were viewed as vital to the proper functioning of the sovereign state. In his article, "A Foucauldian French Revolution?", Baker observes that a Foucauldian interpretation of the Revolution must involve a consideration of the "individualization of human subjects" (191). A consequence of this individualization of human subjects was the production of political subjectivity, involving a "technology of *politicization*" as well (Baker 192). As a result of this process, the actions of each individual were judged to be primary factors of the political sphere. "Each individual was now to be seen as a political actor," Baker writes, "all actions were to be understood as political actions; every phenomenon was to be revealed as the expression of a political will" (192). Recognizing the individual's vital political role was the first step in the politicization of individuals.

A new political subjectivity was born whereby the new political sphere demanded unity of all members of the state so that the general would not be splintered. The principle of indivisibility thus came to the fore. The unified body of the nation came to be identified specifically as "the people." A notion "plus idéale que concrètement désignable" (Jaume 153), the people, like the general will, was also conceptualized in terms of a single, unified entity. Jaume explains that in Jacobin discourse in particular, the people existed as "un individu collectif" whose unity that had to be protected from everything that threatened it (Jaume 154). The unity of the people thus provided Jacobin logic the means for determining the role of the individual in revolutionary society.

Insisting that the people had to be unified in order to legitimize popular sovereignty, the Revolution's leaders disdained expressions of individualism. They were intolerant of any individual will that jeopardized unity because a threat to unity was a threat to sovereignty. "Hence the constant aversion," Baker explains, "to any form of political activity that threatened the unity of the sovereign will by the apparent articulation of particular wills" (Sovereignty 856). Individuals whose private interests were perceived as resting outside the general will could not be part of the social contract between citizens. Those individuals who appeared to maintain their personal interests rather than relinquish them, were regarded as adversaries to the sovereign state. Tension arose between the individual and the collective sovereignty to which one belonged and submitted because of the ambiguous role of the individual – requisite for the political order but incriminated for personal interest (Jaume 155). An adversarial relationship was thus emerged between the public interest and the conflicting individual interest. Robespierre and others frequently referred to this conflict and stressed the preeminence of the public interest over the personal interest. For example, citing "l'amour de la patrie," he stated, "Il est vrai encore que ce sentiment sublime suppose la préférence de l'intérêt public à tous les intérêts particuliers" (10: 353).[5] Because the revolutionaries considered private interests to be in stark contrast to the public interest, the individual was pitted against the political body.

Counterrevolutionary activity was frequently blamed on the perceived differences between the general will and private will. In lambasting the counterrevolution in the Vendée, one orator held private interests accountable for the uprising. Citizen Lacroix stated, "C'est, en un mot, l'intérêt personnel aux prises

---

[5] "It is still true that the sublime sentiment supposes the preference of public interest to all particular interests, whence it follows" (ORFR 371).

avec l'intérêt général" (Markov 102).[6] This is one example of the recurrent rhetoric that differentiated the general will from the private will. It was claimed that private interests disrupted the unitary sovereign will and any expression thereof was to be openly condemned as contrary to the Revolution. Individuals were therefore systematically singled out and denounced in order to preserve the supposed unanimity within the people. The fear of difference, as Baker terms it, generated such a degree of suspicion of private wills that the Revolution's leaders eventually viewed the individual with suspicion. Saint-Just succinctly states this distrust of individual human beings: "Le peuple se trompe: il se trompe moins que les hommes" (521).[7] Revolutionary discourse was often characterized by a sharp polarization attempting to separate the enemies from the people, and isolate the adversarial private wills from the general will. Individuals were synonymous with dissention, and, consequently, were corrupting enemies of the pure French people. The frequent juxtaposition of the terms individual/political body, individual/association, and individual interest/general interest illustrated the rigid opposition between the individual and the people (Barny 68). Barny refers to these opposing terms as "binary groups" that frequently express this antagonism. These antagonisms were articulated recurrently by those in political power, and became increasingly so as the Revolution progressed and became more radicalized. Blum has observed that Jacobin language demonstrated an "ever-shrinking vocabulary," in which, "certain key words: 'virtue,' 'people,' 'pure,' and 'mass,' were contrasted with 'vice,' 'enemies,' 'corrupt,' and 'individuals'" (*Rousseau* 195). Repeatedly, the structure of an utterance reflected this contrast. The use of the *anti-thèse* in rhetoric was constructed so that the people had a certain positive quality but the individual had the negative or opposite characteristic. For example, Robespierre insisted, "Le peuple est sublime mais les individus sont faibles" (9: 559).[8] Saint-Just's speech on

---

[6] "It is, in a word, personal interest battling with the general interest."

[7] "The people are sometimes mistaken, but it is mistaken less than individuals" (*ORFR* 356).

[8] "The people is sublime but individuals are weak."

revolutionary government (October 10, 1793), also provides a good example of this polarizing rhetoric and parallel structure employing the *anti-thèse*. He clearly demarcated the line drawn between the people and its enemies:

> Depuis que le peuple français a manifesté sa volonté, tout ce qui lui est opposé est hors le souverain; tout ce qui est hors le souverain est ennemi. . . . Entre le peuple et ses ennemis il n'y a plus rien de commun que le glaive. (521)[9]

Any individual who dissents from the people's will is not a participant in the people's sovereignty, and is therefore an enemy of the people. Moreover, this enemy is not only a non-participant in the people's will but is detached from the sovereign body politic. Yet one of the great difficulties resided precisely in the determination of the people's will. As those who were sent to the guillotine could readily conclude, the definition of the people's will and opposition to this will was determined by those in political power. From the beginning of the Revolution, invoking the name of the people was necessary in order to legitimize the authority of the revolutionary government, and consequently political orators had to claim to possess the vested authority of the people.[10] A struggle for power was inherent in the struggle to prove that one was speaking for the people and understanding most fully the people's will. Therefore, there great political advantage in declaring that a particular individual was an enemy of the people: it served to validate the speaker's claim to authority. For victims of the Terror, the people's will was defined by the Committee of Public Safety. Anyone who did not agree with the committee risked being identified as an opponent of the people's will and thus being outside the sovereign body. These enemies paid the price with their heads on the guillotine. Thus liberty for individuals

---

[9] "For, since the French people has manifested its will, all that is opposed to it is outside the sovereign, all that is outside the sovereign is the enemy . . . between the people and its enemies there is no longer anything in common but the sword" (*ORFR* 355).

[10] As Hunt explains, "Language becomes an expression of power, and power is expressed by the right to speak for the people" (Politics 23).

was assured as long as those in power determined that their private interests conformed to those of the abstract general will.

The trial of Louis XVI was one of the earliest, most striking examples of the Revolution's polarizing distinction between the rights of an individual and those of the people. In fact, the king was the first person to be executed as an "enemy of the people" during the Revolution (Blum, Rousseau 256). His trial exemplifies how the abstract notions of the individual came into conflict with the reality of an individual's concrete existence.

The speech that Saint-Just delivered to the National Convention during the judging of the king (November 13, 1792) was a defining moment early in this revolutionary's political career. Not only was it an influential speech that would earn him renown on the political stage, but it also set forth principles concerning the individual that would persist throughout the Terror and the remaining years of his own life. On the one hand, he insisted on presenting the king as an abstract entity that embodied opposition to the people. On the other hand, both he and Robespierre argued that it was the king's physical existence that represented a threat to the survival of the sovereign nation. Robespierre maintained that the trial should not focus on a verdict pronouncing the guilt or innocence of the king, but should be concerned with demonstrating how the existence of this individual threatened the nation. He declared, "Vous n'avez point une sentence à rendre pour ou contre un homme; mais une mesure de salut public à prendre, un acte de providence nationale à exercer. . . . Louis doit mourir parce qu'il faut que la patrie vive" (9: 121, 130).[11] He referred to the idea that under a monarchy, sovereignty resided in the king's individual self, and to destroy this body was to destroy monarchical sovereignty in favor of popular sovereignty. The king was an enemy of the people, and this in itself was the crime of which he was guilty. Saint-Just abstractly assigned to Louis'

---

[11] "You do not have a verdict to give for or against a man, but a measure to take for the public safety, a precautionary act to execute for the nation . . . . Louis must die because the nation must live" (*ORFR* 307, 311).

individual self the violence against the people that was committed in defense of the monarchy during confrontations such as those at the Bastille, Champ-de-Mars, and the Tuilieries. He called Louis, "un homme assassin d'un peuple, pris en flagrant délit, la main dans le sang, la main dans le crime!" (377).[12] But Saint-Just did not wish to try him for having physically perpetrated such crimes; the king was not accused of the crime of murder or for directing the deaths per se during the Champ-de-Mars massacre or other violent episodes. Rather, he was simply guilty of royalty, "culpable by metaphysical category" (Blum, *Rousseau* 224). His guilt was implicit in his reign: "On ne peut point régner innocemment" (Saint-Just 379).[13]

Saint-Just's contribution to the debates concerning the trial was his characterization of the king as, precisely, an enemy of the French people. In previous debates it had been frequently suggested, particularly by the Girondins, that the king be tried as a citizen and according to the constitutional dictates of legal procedure. Condorcet, for example, had proposed that Louis' crimes "peuvent être jugés et punis comme les crimes de la même espèce, commis par un autre individu" (*Archives* 54: 149).[14] Saint-Just, however, objected to granting the king the status of ordinary citizen: "L'unique but du Comité [de législation] fut de vous persuader que le roi devait être jugé en simple citoyen; et moi, je dis que le roi doit être jugé en ennemi" (376).[15] This argument was based on the principle that the king was not and never had been a participant in the social contract between citizens. This was an innovative idea, for Saint-Just denied that the king had ever been a member of the French people (Walzer 62). And if one was not a member of the people, one was an enemy of the people. The king accordingly should be denied a trial governed by the civil laws which emanate from the general will of citizens within the social contract. Since the

---

[12] " . . . a man who was the assassin of a people, taken *in flagrante*, his hand soaked with blood, his hand plunged in crime" (*ORFR* 304).

[13] "No man can reign innocently" (*ORFR* 306).

[14] *Archives parlementaires* will be abbreviated *AP* henceforth.

[15] "The single aim of the committee was to persuade you that the king should be judged as an ordinary citizen. And I say that the king should be judged as an enemy" (*ORFR* 304).

king had no part in this contract, the laws applying to the people could not also be applied to him. Thus in Louis' case, these laws were invalid (Blum, *Rousseau* 175). Saint-Just explains,

> Les citoyens se lient par le contrat; le souverain ne se lie pas. . . . Le pacte est un contrat entre les citoyens, et non point avec le gouvernement: on n'est pour rien dans un contrat où l'on ne s'est point obligé. Conséquemment Louis, qui ne s'était pas obligé ne peut pas être jugé civilement. (378)[16]

Situated outside the social contract and in opposition to the general will, the king had no right to a legal trial. It was because of this exteriority that he was guilty. Therefore, Saint-Just stated, he must be punished: "Pour moi, il n'y a point de milieu: cet homme doit régner ou mourir" (378).[17]

Saint-Just asserted that in order for Louis to be executed without a trial, he could not merely be like any other man guilty of a crime, as Condorcet had proposed. He had to be identified and declared an outsider, excluded from the social contract which binds citizens within the unity of the sovereign will. Because of this notion of the sovereign will, the revolutionaries constantly sought "to achieve unity by way of exclusion" (Baker, Sovereignty 856). Saint-Just condemned the king by excluding him from this unified citizenry, and he unified the citizenry by excluding the monarch. He emphasized that the king was not one of them. He called him "un étranger parmi nous" (380); he wanted to prove that the king "doit être jugé comme un ennemi étranger" (381); and he demanded, "quel ennemi, quel étranger nous a fait plus de mal?" (381).[18] Here, Saint-Just effectively eliminated the king rhetorically from the body of the French people, and in so doing, he prepared the way for him to mount the scaffold for his execution.

---

[16] "The citizens are bound by the contract; the sovereign is not... The social contract is between citizen and citizen, not between citizen and government. A contract affects only those whom it binds. As a consequence, Louis, who was not bound, cannot not be judged in civil law" (*ORFR* 305).

[17] "For myself, I can see no mean: this man must reign or die" (*ORFR* 305).

[18] " . . . an alien among us;" " . . . must be judged as a foreign enemy;" "what enemy, what alien has done us more harm?" (*ORFR* 307).

The reasoning of Saint-Just's speech resonated in the year to follow. Characterizing the individual as a menace to unity meant that the individual was labelled an enemy or outsider. Robespierre effectively excluded enemies from citizenship in the Republic with an argument similar to the one used by Saint-Just during the king's trial. Saint-Just denied that the king was a member of the French people, and Robespierre extended this denial to royalists and "conspirators" as well. He accordingly narrowed the scope of citizenship by stating that, "Il n'y a de citoyens dans la République que les républicains. Les royalistes, les conspirateurs ne sont, pour elle, que des étrangers, ou plutôt des ennemis" (10: 357).[19] These so-called non-citizens, like the king, had no protection from the law since the law was not applicable to those who disrupted the people's unity. The term "individual" thus acquired a pejorative connotation in Jacobin discourse, and in the writings of Billaud-Varenne particularly (Jaume 190). In Eléments du républicanisme, he makes a sharp, albeit contradictory, distinction between the individual and the citizen. In fact, he explicitly states, "Dans tout Etat civilisé, la première nuance que l'on découvre présente deux classes d'hommes bien distincts: les citoyens et les individus" (AP 67: 224).[20] Citizens, according to Billaud-Varenne, place the public interest above their own and work solely for the good of the country: "Les citoyens sont ceux qui, pénétrés des devoirs sociaux, rapportent tout à l'intérêt public et qui mettent leur bonheur et leur gloire à cimenter la prospérité de leur pays" (AP 67: 224).[21] The citizen is of course an individual, but one whose identity is not tied to expressions of individuality. The citizen is rather a "citoyen-individu," as Jaume terms it, who is only one fraction of the sovereign and does not appear as an entity distinct from the general will (179). Individuals, on the other hand, are distinguished from the general

---

[19] "There are no citizens in the Republic but the republicans. The royalists, the conspirators are, in its eyes, only strangers, or rather, enemies" (ORFR 375).
[20] "In every civilized state, the first nuance that one discovers presents two distinct categories: citizens and individuals."
[21] "Citizens are those who, imbued with their sense of social duty, yield everything to the public interest and who place their own happiness and glory into fortifying the prosperity of their country."

will because of their self-imposed isolation from the social body. They strive not for the public good but for their own personal well-being. Billaud-Varenne writes that individuals are "ceux qui s'isolent, ou plutôt qui savent moins travailler au bien public que calculer leur profit particulier" (*AP* 67: 224).[22] Their personal interest has negative repercussions on the public interest because they "cherchent à rompre l'équilibre de l'égalité, pour accroître leur bien-être personnel en usurpant celui des autres" (*AP* 67: 224).[23] The paradoxical reasoning here is that a people constituting the general will is comprised of individual citizens, but not of individuals. Citizens are those good and virtuous individuals who throw off their demands of individuality and wrap themselves in the pursuit of the public good. The individual, however, not to be equated with the citizen, poses a threat to the equality enjoyed under popular sovereignty. The citizenry by definition has to be unified in its will. A new category of individuals therefore had to be created – the adversarial non-citizen.

Identifying the individual

In order to eliminate adversaries, as the trial of the king demonstrated, the revolutionaries first had to condemn them by means of a rhetoric that established their status as non-citizens. Once they had removed individual enemies from the body politic in an abstract sense, those in political power were forced to follow up on their rhetoric with actions, and were confronted with the concrete existence of such individuals. This process, whereby the accusatory rhetoric becomes the overriding means by which enemies are eliminated from the unified body politic, played a key role in the Revolution's increasingly radical direction. Blum describes this tendency as the redefinition of the body politic, a process whereby groups are eliminated from the body politic "by words before their destruction in the flesh"

---

[22] " . . . those who are isolated, or rather, who know less how to work toward the public good than to calculate their own profit."

[23] " . . . seek to disrupt the equilibrium of equality in order to increase their personal well-being by usurping that of others."

(*Representing* 133). The Revolution was therefore increasingly radicalized as those in power sought to make it consistent with their discourse (Furet 98).

The revolutionaries had to be vigilant in identifying any individual or group of individuals who might jeopardize the unity of the body politic. They alleged that to permit discord was to put the Revolution and the nation – or *la patrie* – in danger. Therefore the discovery of possible sources of discord was vital to the survival of the sovereign nation. When Danton, the Minister of Justice at the time, suggested revolutionary measures, including "visites domiciliaires" (August 28, 1792), he justified this tactic by claiming, "Tout appartient à la patrie, quand la patrie est en danger" (116).[24] Although his demand was originally for the search of firearms, the domiciliary visits led more often than not to a search for suspected persons (Schama 626). In fact, one of the most notorious practices adopted during the Revolution was precisely the application of extensive mechanisms for keeping watch over citizens and their actions in order to detect any counterrevolutionary activity.

This surveillance was officially instituted on March 21, 1793, with the creation of the watch committees, or *comités de surveillance*. Danton had proposed this committee on January 21 of that year, requesting that, "ils aient le droit de se faire ouvrir telle maison où ils pourraient penser qu'on recèle un conspirateur" (Stephens 186).[25] The wording of the official order on March 21 therefore stipulated that the committees keep watch over activities of foreigners, their place of residence, their "sentiments civiques," and participation in riots (*AP* 60: 389). Moreover, each citizen over age eighteen, too, had to declare his performance of his civic duties ("l'acquit de ses devoirs civiques") (*AP* 60: 389-90). This order was eventually broadened to cover all suspected persons, not just foreigners. The Law of Suspects in September of that year expanded the watch committees' powers and made them responsible for drawing up lists of all suspected persons and issuing warrants of

---

[24] "Everything belongs to the homeland when the homeland is in danger."
[25] " . . . they have the right to open homes where they believe a conspirator is hiding."

arrests against them: "Les comités de surveillance . . . sont chargés de dresser, chacun dans son arrondissement, la liste des gens suspects" (*AP* 74: 304).[26] The increase in the power of the *comités de surveillance* in article three of the law was due in part to the purpose stated in the order's preamble. The original overall mission of the committees was quite broad and clearly could justify an expansion of powers. The preamble announced that the National Convention wished to give these committees, "tous les moyens d'éclairer le mal et d'en arrêter les progrès" (*AP* 60: 389).[27] This "*mal*" was defined in terms of individuals whose words and deeds did not coincide with the general will. The order stated that the National Convention "doit en redoublant de surveillance, empêcher que les ennemis de l'intérieur ne parviennent à étouffer le voeu des patriotes, et ne substituent des volontés privées à la volonté générale" (*AP* 60: 389).[28] In spite of both the 1791 and June 1793 constitutions' guarantees of freedom of opinion,[29] the establishment of legal surveillance committees and the Law of Suspects made the *salut du peuple* a "supreme law that preempted civil rights" (Kennedy 313). In other words, not all individuals enjoyed the liberty that was guaranteed – only those individuals whose words and deeds coincided with revolutionary ideals. The watch committees, along with agents in the Ministry of the Interior whose task it was to eavesdrop on citizens (Kennedy 313), prevented individuals from freely expressing an opinion that could be interpreted as a "private interest." Like the panopticon, the watch committees guaranteed only that individuals would be closely observed.

---

[26] "The Watch Committees . . . are charged with drafting, each in its own arrondissement, a list of suspected persons" (Stewart 478).

[27] " . . . every means of watching evil and of checking the progress thereof" (Stewart 412).

[28] "It must, in redoubling surveillance, prevent the internal enemies from succeeding in stifling the will of the patriots and substituting private interests for the general will" (Stewart 412).

[29] The constitution of 1791 states, "Tout citoyen peut donc parler, écrire, imprimer librement" (*AP* 30: 152) ["Liberty to every man to speak, write, print, and publish his opinions" (Stewart 232).] The constitution of June 1793 was suspended indefinitely and was never put into effect. Nevertheless, it states, "Le droit de manifester sa pensée et ses opinions, soit par la voie de la presse, soit de toute autre manière . . . ne peuvent être interdits" (*AP* 67: 143) ["The right of manifesting ideas and opinions, either through the press or in any other manner . . . may not be forbidden" (Stewart 456).].

The drive to discover and expose private wills and individual interests forced the Jacobins to form new and expanded definitions of the enemy. New meanings had to be created in order to facilitate the identification and removal of supposed enemies of the Revolution. While a distinction between the people and its enemies was made consistently, the designation of this enemy constantly changed. Blum explains: "The original dichotomy between the good innocent ones and the wicked who deserved to die continued unchanged, although the identities of the latter changed with each round of executions" (*Rousseau* 261). In the early phase of the Revolution the enemies of liberty were easily distinguished as belonging to the monarchy and the nobility. Soon, the evil enemies were no longer just the defenders of the old order; each individual who expressed a personal interest now joined their ranks (Jaume 169). Divisions within the Assembly and the Convention forced competing groups to go on the attack and deny that their political foes were in conformity with the people's will. In order to justify their attacks, they limited the category of the people and enlarged the category of the enemy. As Baker explains,

> The logic of a unitary sovereign will, intensified by war and internal division required constant elimination of difference through the progressive expansion of the category of "aristocracy" and corresponding restriction of the category of "nation" or "people." (Sovereignty 856)

An example of this expansion of the category of aristocracy is found in the proceedings of the National Convention on September 5, 1793, the day usually taken to mark the beginning of the Reign of Terror. A Parisian crowd consisting of delegations from the Paris Commune and from the Jacobin Club marched on the Convention and famously demanded, "Placez la terreur à l'ordre du jour"[30] (*Moniteur* 17: 586). In response to their demands, the president of the Convention told the

---

[30] Nearly all English translations of this infamous demand are, "Make terror the order of the day" (for example, see *ORFR* 350). I believe that a better translation would be, "Place terror on the agenda."

delegation that indeed, all enemies must cease to exist. He linked the enemies to the aristocracy:

> La liberté survivra aux intrigues et aux projets des conspirateurs . . . . La terre de la liberté, souillée par la présence de ses ennemis, va en être affranchie. Aujourd'hui leur arrêt de mort est prononcé, et demain l'aristocratie cessera d'être. (*Moniteur* 17: 581)[31]

In this context, the term "aristocracy" did not actually refer to aristocrats but anyone who was not favorable to the Revolution. The inclusion of greater numbers of people under labels that highlighted differences enabled the revolutionaries to rid themselves of opposing forces.

The struggle for power in the first half of 1793 typifies the use of the expanded classification of the people's enemies. The victory of the Jacobins and fatal defeat of the Girondins at the end of May 1793 was due in part to the swelling category of enemy status. In order to purge the Convention of the Girondins, the Jacobins had to portray them as traitors to the nation of citizens. Such traitors had to be purged from the Convention because, as Baker explains, it was necessary that the assembly be unified just as the people was unified; the assembly's unity emanated from the people's unity (Sovereignty 856). Marat wrote in his paper *Publiciste de la république française,* in April 1793, "Le foyer de toutes les conspirations contre la patrie est au sein de la Convention" (9: 5994).[32] At the heart of this conspiracy were, "infidèles," "vils intrigants," and, "scélérats" (9: 5994). These pronouncements established a wide range of terms that incorporated a wide range of enemies. No longer described only as aristocrats or royalists, the enemies now were called unfaithful, vile scoundrels.

---

[31] "Liberty will outlive the intrigues and schemes of conspirators . . . . The land of liberty, sullied by the presences of its enemies, is going to be freed from them. Today their death sentence is pronounced, and tomorrow aristocracy will cease to exist" (*ORFR* 346).

[32] "The center of all the conspiracies against the homeland is within the Convention."

The purge of the Girondins exposed how distinguishing the individual foe from the people served to protect and promote one's own political power. Eliminating the enemy became an effective means of securing political survival. An inflammatory circular from the Paris Jacobin Club to other branches of the club called for the purge of the Girondins that would prevent the Jacobins' own political defeat. The circular, which included the signature of Marat, demanded action: "Mettons en état d'arrestation tous les ennemies de notre révolution et toutes les personnes suspectes. Exterminons, sans pitié, tous les conspirateurs, si nous ne voulons être exterminés nous-mêmes" (9: 6025).[33] If the Jacobins failed to arrest and subsequently eliminate each enemy, it warned, they themselves would be eliminated. Danton had previously sounded the alarm that the *patrie* was in danger; now the Jacobins cried out that disunity placed them in danger.

In September of 1793 the Jacobins sought to provide a legal definition of individuals whose actions were determined to be a threat to the Revolution. The Law of Suspects (September 17, 1793) offered very broad descriptions of suspected persons. As a result, its terms were ultimately quite vague. It stipulated that anyone who did not overtly support the Revolution could be considered suspicious. Or as Weber has written, the law cast such a wide net that "every citizen ran the risk of falling into it, just by virtue of being an individual" (109). The second article of this law listed six definitions of suspects the first of which was, "ceux qui, soit par leur conduite, soit par leurs relations, soit par leurs propos ou leurs écrits, se sont montrés partisans de la tyrannie ou de fédéralisme, et ennemis de la liberté" (*AP* 74: 303).[34] Deciphering the exact meanings of "partisan of tyranny" and "enemy of liberty" was impossible because these terms were clearly subjective. Furthermore, former nobles and their family members "qui n'ont pas constamment manifesté leur attachement à

---

[33] "Let us arrest all enemies of our revolution and all suspected persons. Let us exterminate, without pity, all conspirators unless we want to be exterminated ourselves."

[34] " . . . those who, by their conduct, associations, talk, or writings have shown themselves partisans of tyranny or federalism and enemies of liberty" (Stewart 478).

la Révolution" were also suspected persons (*AP* 74: 303).[35] Individuals falling under this category were faced with the difficulty of proving a negative – that they did not *not* support the Revolution. Nevertheless legal rhetoric such as this would provide guidelines for separating the supposed virtuous individuals – those who loved the nation and its laws, according to Robespierre – from the enemies who would in turn pay the price of their treason with their lives. "In demanding a Law of Suspects," Baker explains, "the sans-culottes were in effect insisting that the Convention purge the people . . . of all elements of disunity" (Sovereignty 856).

As definitions of the enemy continued to expand after the Law of Suspects, the Terror became progressively more repressive toward the individual. In October 1793, when a revolutionary government was declared and the constitution suspended, Saint-Just proposed that individuals be considered traitorous not only for counterrevolutionary activity but also for the *lack* of revolutionary activity. He announced to the National Convention, "Vous avez à punir non seulement les traîtres, mais les indifférents mêmes; vous avez à punir quiconque est passif dans la République et ne fait rien pour elle" (521).[36] Henceforth, an individual's inaction and lack of patriotic enthusiasm was dangerous to the Republic.

Definitions of the enemy such as these provided very little leeway for accused individuals. Saint-Just proclaimed that justice was not to be troubled with individual interests: "Toutefois, il faut être juste; mais au lieu de l'être conséquemment à l'intérêt particulier, il faut l'être conséquemment à l'intérêt public" (698).[37] Robespierre echoed Saint-Just's stance on the dispensing of justice. He too refused to guarantee fairness towards declared enemies and in his speech on revolutionary government (December 25, 1793), he argued, "Le gouvernement révolutionnaire doit aux bons citoyens toute la protection nationale; il ne doit aux ennemis du peuple que

---

[35] " . . . who have not steadily manifested their devotion to the Revolution" (Stewart 478).

[36] "You have to punish not only the traitors, but even those who are indifferent; you have to punish whoever is passive in the republic, and who does nothing for it" (*ORFR* 355).

[37] "However, one must be just; but instead of being so for individual interest, one must be so for the public interest."

la mort" (10: 274).[38] The protection of the law was granted only to those who collaborated in the government's policies; those who did not were enemies of the Republic who deserved only death (Bouloiseau 109). The formal declaration of a revolutionary government confirmed this principle. As Robespierre described it, the purpose of a constitutional government was to preserve what had been established, a goal that included protection of the individual from abuses of the state. On the other hand, the purpose of a revolutionary government was not to preserve civil liberties but to establish a republic. Robespierre described the difference between a constitutional government and a revolutionary government in the following manner:

> Le gouvernement constitutionnel s'occupe principalement de la liberté civile: et le gouvernement révolutionnaire, de la liberté publique. Sous le régime constitutionnel, il suffit presque de protéger les individus contre l'abus de la puissance publique: sous le régime révolutionnaire, la puissance publique elle-même est obligée de se défendre contre toutes les factions qui l'attaquent. (10: 274)[39]

The duty of the revolutionary government that directed the Terror was not to protect the individual from abuses of the state but to protect the state from abuses of individuals.

The Law of 22 Prairial (June 10, 1794) accelerated the speed with which the Revolutionary Tribunal could send the people's enemies to the guillotine. The original purpose of the Revolutionary Tribunal was precisely to create a mechanism whereby individuals who were guilty of causing disunity could be quickly condemned. The decree establishing this court (March 10, 1793) charged it with trying cases of counterrevolutionary activities, which included all attacks upon

---

[38] "The revolutionary government owes its full protection to good citizens; to enemies of the people, it owes only death."

[39] "Constitutional government is principally concerned with civil liberty, and revolutionary government with public liberty. Under a constitutional regime, it is nearly sufficient to protect individuals against the abuse of power by the state: under a revolutionary regime, it is the state which has to defend itself against all the factions that attack it."

unity.[40] The quick resolution of these cases was facilitated with the passing of the Law of 22 Prairial. Practices that would ensure the fairness of a trial were abandoned. The law denied the accused the right of counsel, permitted hearsay as evidence, and sentenced all offenders to death. It was not, as are most courts, instituted to judge the accused (Blum, *Rousseau* 256). It was a foregone conclusion that the accused were guilty. Instead, the Tribunal was specifically charged with punishing the people's enemies (*AP* 91: 484). In the same vague terms that previous definitions of the enemies had provided, the law stipulated that, "Les ennemis du peuple sont ceux qui cherchent à anéantir la liberté publique, soit par la force, soit par la ruse" (*AP* 91: 484).[41] In addition, enemies were, "Ceux qui auront secondé les projets des ennemis de la France," and included those who "auront attenté à la liberté, à l'unité, à la sûreté de la République, ou travaillé à en empêcher l'affermissement" (*AP* 91: 484).[42] Whether or not an individual committed one of the crimes listed here, such as an attack on liberty, was open to interpretation due to the lack of a clear definition and the abstractness of such a crime. "These crimes were nothing less than metaphysical murders," Blum points out, "all the more awesome as they were intangible: liberticide and patricide" (*Rousseau* 257). The intangibility of these crimes made it nearly impossible for individuals to defend themselves before the tribunal. Nevertheless they were to mount the scaffold as the physical embodiment of a private will detached from the general will.

The survival of the new order thrived on the scrutiny of individuals who posed a threat to the nation and one particularly effective means of singling out

---

[40] The first article of the decree for the Revolutionary Tribunal began, "Il sera établi à Paris un tribunal criminel extraordinaire, qui connaîtra de toute entreprise contre-révolutionnaire, de tous attentats contre la liberté, l'égalité, l'unité . . . " (Duvergier 5: 190). ["An extraordinary criminal tribunal will be established in Paris. It will have jurisdiction over all counterrevolutionary operations, over all attacks on liberty, equality, unity . . . ."]

[41] "The enemies of the people are those who seek to destroy public liberty, either by force or by cunning" (Stewart 528).

[42] "Those who have supported the designs of the enemies of France . . . have made an attempt against the liberty, unity, and security of the Republic, or labored to prevent the strengthening thereof" (Stewart 529).

enemies was the practice of denunciation. Jaume, who has written extensively on the subject, calls it the pursuit of the individual (192). Motivated by fears of foreign plots and internal factions, revolutionary orators and journalists alike took part in the public and systematic naming of individuals whom they suspected of harboring counterrevolutionary intentions. Although the practice of denunciation was not unique to the Jacobins, it did play a key role in their political subjectification of the individual. The Jacobins were consumed with the idea that individuals had hidden agendas that needed to be exposed. Specifically, they asserted that the enemies were "masked" as patriots, and must be "unmasked" as the traitors they really were. Denouncing them was one successful method of unmasking them. In both speeches and published materials, terms such as *dénoncer, démasquer, déjouer*, and *dévoiler* appeared with noticeable frequency.

Public denunciations of suspected individuals were widespread, especially in Marat's newspapers, which made a habit of denunciations.[43] In fact Marat describes the aim of his *Journal de la République française* as one of, "dévoiler les complots, démasquer les traîtres" (8: 4753).[44] He continuously and predictably filled his paper with accusations of traitorous activity and speech, of conspiracy, and of counterrevolutionary deeds. He described his suspicions in great depth, verbally attacking those individuals whom he suspected of being enemies of liberty and of the people. In November 1792 he defended his denunciations by explaining that they were necessary to prevent the *patrie* from falling. Denouncing individuals was therefore an integral part of the task of securing public liberty: "Le salut du peuple étant la loi suprême de l'Etat, la porte doit être ouverte à toute dénonciation" (8: 5053).[45] By opening the door to denunciations, the revolutionaries facilitated the individualization of political enemies while at the same time condemning them in the

---

[43] While Marat is most famous for the paper entitled *L'Ami du peuple*, he changed the title to *Journal de la République française* in 1792, and then to *Publiciste de la République française*.
[44] " . . . remove the veil from plots, unmask the traitors."
[45] "The safety of the people being the supreme law of the state, the door must be open to all denunciations."

name of universal principles (Baker 192). Naming the enemy was the equivalent of eliminating and punishing the traitor. According to Marat, "Nommer ces traîtres ... c'est prononcer la punition qu'ils méritent" (8: 5113).[46] It was precisely when individuals were identified that they were rhetorically – and eventually physically – eliminated from the body politic.

Revolutionary denunciations not only enabled the identification of enemies, they also constituted a civic duty for ensuring the safety of the *patrie*. In March, 1794, Saint-Just proposed a decree to the Convention that would require private citizens to denounce publicly anyone who was conspiring against the republic. This proposal was adopted as part of the Law of 22 Prairial. The law stated, "Tout citoyen a le droit de saisir et de traduire devant les magistrats les conspirateurs et les contre-révolutionnaires. Il est tenu de les dénoncer dès qu'il les connoît" (*AP* 91: 484).[47] As private citizens were asked to unmask and denounce suspects, they were called upon to participate in the official surveillance that subjectified individuals in the political sphere. Denunciation thus became the "democratization of surveillance" (Baker 200). In fact, as Baker writes, "The denouncer had the right, and obligation, to expose the obscure treacheries of each and every individual to the light of the new political panopticon" (200). The individual was therefore an object of intense scrutiny, and the only individuals who could emerge unscathed were those deemed to be virtuous citizens.

The virtuous individual?

According to Rousseau, a nation of virtuous citizens is born when individuals surrender their wills to the general will. In this ideal society, virtue is determined by participation in the general will, and vice, by one's detachment from it. Rousseau defines virtue in *Economie politique* as conformity with the general will: "Tout

---

[46] "Naming these traitors ... is pronouncing the punishment they deserve."
[47] "Every citizen has the right to seize conspirators and counter-revolutionaries, and to arraign them before the magistrates. He is required to denounce them as soon as he knows of them" (Stewart 530).

homme est vertueux quand sa volonté particulière est conforme en tout à la volonté générale" (254).[48] In this context, virtue has a political significance. The dichotomy between virtuous and non-virtuous citizens reflects the dichotomy between the people and its enemies. The enemies of the people are not only traitors to the *patrie*, they are evil and immoral individuals. They have placed their own wills above the general will rather than within it. Because these unvirtuous individuals disrupt the unity of the sovereign nation, the government must be committed to enforcing political virtue in order to maintain a unified body politic. Individual virtue is a vital element in the successful functioning of the state, and the legislator must see to it that virtue reigns. As Rousseau put it, "Faites régner la vertu" (*Economie* 252).[49] Robespierre in particular sought to establish this reign of virtue.

Robespierre was famously consumed with securing a republic of virtuous individuals. He wanted a political morality that was inseparable from politics and was not derived from traditional religious dictates. His ideas and his utterances on republican political virtue closely resembled those of Rousseau.[50] Like Rousseau, he associated the concept of virtue with that of the general will and conceptualized virtue in terms of one's contribution to the well-being of the *patrie*. Furthermore, love for one's country was also a factor in affirming one's virtue. Rousseau had written, "Voulons-nous que les peuples soient vertueux? Commençons donc par leur faire aimer la patrie" (*Economie* 255).[51] Approximately forty years later, in a speech delivered in February 1794, Robespierre spoke of a virtuous love for *la patrie* as well: "Je parle de la vertu publique . . . qui n'est autre chose que l'amour de la Patrie et de ses lois" (10: 353).[52]

---

[48] "Every man is virtuous when his particular will is in all things conformable to the general will" (142).

[49] "Make virtue reign."

[50] According to George Rudé, Robespierre's ideas concerning republican virtue were influenced most strongly by Rousseau (96).

[51] "Do you wish men to be virtuous? Then let us begin by making them love their country" (143).

[52] "I speak of the public virtue . . . which is nothing other than the love of the nation and its laws" (*ORFR* 371).

This famous speech on political morality articulated the principles that he believed were essential for the proper administration of the republic. It was representative of Robespierre's political thought and of the "fundamental truths to which he remained unswervingly attached" (Rudé 95). Among these fundamental truths was the idea that virtue, an indispensable component in the republic, constituted the soul of the Republic – "l'âme de la République" (10: 354). He maintained that virtue was "le principe fondamental du gouvernement démocratique ou populaire, c'est-à-dire, le ressort essentiel qui le soutien et qui le fait mouvoir" (10: 353).[53] Without virtue, there could be no republic, because, "Dans le système de la révolution française . . . ce qui est corrupteur est contre-révolutionnaire" (10: 354).[54] Unvirtuous individuals were counterrevolutionary and had to be removed from the body politic. The republic had to be purified and left uncontaminated of evil individuals whose private interests superseded the public good. Whether they were conducted against the royalists, Girondists, Hébertists, or Dantonists, purges to separate the evil ones from the virtuous citizens were part of the continuing quest for absolute purity (Blum, *Rousseau* 226, 200). A sharp distinction was drawn between vice and virtue. One fell either on the side of virtue or on the side of vice; and those who were not on the side of virtue were victims of the Terror.

Terror was in fact oddly related to virtue. Robespierre characterized terror as a derivative of virtue because it enforced a stern but virtuous justice on evil-doers. He wanted to institutionalize terror as an instrument of government, but believed that for terror to be just, it had to be tempered with virtue (Rudé 118). Virtue and terror were interdependent in time of revolution: virtue was worthless without the unyielding justice of terror, and terror was unduly repressive without the moderating influence of virtue. For Robespierre, virtue and terror were inextricably linked:

---

[53] " . . . the fundamental principle of popular or democratic government, that is to say, the essential mainspring which sustains it and makes it move" (*ORFR* 371).

[54] "Within the scheme of the French revolution . . . that which is corrupting is counter-revolutionary" (*ORFR* 372).

> Le ressort du gouvernement populaire en révolution est à la fois la
> vertu et la terreur: la vertu, sans laquelle la terreur est funeste; la
> terreur, sans laquelle la vertu est impuissante. La terreur n'est autre
> chose que la justice prompte, sévère, inflexible; elle est donc une
> émanation de la vertu. (10: 357)[55]

According to Robespierre, political virtue required that the people's enemies be
governed by terror. Terror, among whose mechanisms were the Revolutionary
Tribunal, the Law of Suspects, and punishment by death on the guillotine, could only
be meted out to specific persons who were judged to be unvirtuous.

Whereas virtue was depicted as belonging to an abstract *peuple*, vice was an
attribute of individuals. When Robespierre claimed, "Heureusement la vertu est
naturelle au peuple" (10: 355),[56] he by no means intended to imply that individuals
were virtuous as well. He had stated several years earlier that liberty would be
strengthened if only "les individus étoient aussi purs que la masse de la nation" (5:
304).[57] The nation was pure, yet individuals had to become so. Virtuous individuals
needed to be formed. At issue was the question of determining how, exactly,
individuals were to be transformed into citizens inclined to place the general interest
of the society above their own (Jaume 158).

The legislator was given the task of seeing to it that individuals be imbued
with virtue and learn to love the *patrie*. Blum has effectively argued that Robespierre
defined his role as a legislator in the Rousseauian sense. Rousseau proposed in his
Du contrat social that the legislator be a guide with a superior intelligence and be
able to "transformer chaque individu" (65).[58] Robespierre indeed wanted to
transform each individual into a virtuous citizen. This was the principal subject of
his morality speech and became the goal of the Terror. He exhorted the legislators

---

[55] "The mainspring of popular government in peacetime is virtue, amid revolution it is at the same time
[both] virtue and terror: virtue, without which terror is fatal; terror, without which virtue is impotent.
Terror is nothing but prompt, severe, inflexible justice; it is therefore an emanation of virtue" (*ORFR*
374).
[56] "Happily virtue is natural to the people" (*ORFR* 373).
[57] " . . . individuals were as pure as the mass of the nation."
[58] " . . . transforming each individual" (213).

of the Convention to conduct themselves in a manner that would lead to the "développement de la vertu" (10: 354). Just as Rousseau had declared that citizens must be taught to be good, Robespierre also stated that civic morality had to be imposed from above. In May of 1791 he contended that, "Le premier devoir du législateur est de former et de conserver les moeurs politiques, source de toute liberté, source de tout bonheur social" (7: 439).[59] He would more fully develop this idea of constructing political morality as the Revolution wore on and as he gained more power within the Convention and the Committee of Public Safety. In his last address to the Convention, just one day before his arrest, he clearly stated his belief that civic goodness was to be dictated: "Les autres révolutions n'exigeaient que de l'ambition; la nôtre *impose des vertus*" (emphasis added; 10: 544).[60] The Cult of the Supreme Being was one means to attempt to impose virtue.

The Cult of the Supreme Being as Robespierre envisioned it was to be a civic religion that would celebrate republican ideals. Religious devotion would be directed towards a deity that smiled upon liberty, equality and republican virtue. At the Festival of the Supreme Being (June 8, 1794) Robespierre proclaimed to the French people, "Peuple, livrons-nous aujourd'hui, sous ses auspices, aux transports d'une pure allégresse; demain . . . nous donnerons au monde l'exemple des vertus républicaines, et ce sera l'honorer encore" (10: 482).[61] Resembling more a sermon than a speech, this discourse demonstrated that Robespierre saw himself as a guide to the people and meant to lead them not only towards a particular political destiny but to a virtuous state of being as well. The ultimate goal of the Revolution, he had said several months earlier, was to enjoy "le règne de cette justice éternelle, dont les

---

[59] "The first duty of the legislator is to form and to conserve public morals, source of all liberty, source of all social happiness."

[60] "Other revolutions demanded only ambition; ours imposes virtue."

[61] "People, let us surrender ourselves today, under his auspices, to the just ecstasy of pure joy. Tomorrow... we will give the world an example of republican virtues: and that will honor the Divinity more" (*ORFR* 387).

lois ont été gravées, non sur le marbre ou sur la pierre, mais dans les coeurs de tous les hommes" (10: 352).[62] It was his duty to secure this goal.

The role of inscribing eternal justice into everyone's heart was a primary function of good government. In the past, according to Robespierre, the art of governing was, "l'art de tromper et de corrompre les hommes," but in fact, "il ne doit être que celui de les éclairer et de les rendre meilleurs" (10: 445).[63] In other words, the art of governing, as Foucault points out, involves focusing on the details of individuals' lives and conduct. This pastoral kind of power was embraced by the Jacobin leaders. It would enable them, they thought, to shape individual citizens into what they needed to be in order to keep the revolutionary government alive and to ensure a republican future. "Le législateur commande à l'avenir," Saint-Just declared, "C'est à lui de rendre les hommes ce qu'il veut qu'ils soient" (418).[64] Clearly, Saint-Just saw his role as one that had the power to modify the behavior and will of each citizen.

The implementation of virtue and the turning of individuals into what a legislator wanted them to be proved to be more difficult in practice than the theory suggested. Not only did such a theory require political individualization of citizens, it also required an understanding and appreciation of the uniqueness of each individual. It was the latter of these requirements that the Jacobin leaders failed to grasp. They had singled out individuals as enemies in order to remove the corrupt counterrevolutionary elements. They criticized the private will in order to promote their own interpretation of the general will. But they balked when it came to extending pity and justice towards individuals. As Saint-Just said in a report to the Convention, "Vous avez donc moins à décider de ce qui importe à tel ou tel individu, qu'à décider de ce qui importe à la République; moins à céder aux vues privées, qu'à

---

[62] "The reign of that eternal justice whose laws have been inscribed, not in marble or stone, but in the hearts of all men" (*ORFR* 370).

[63] " . . . the art of deceiving and corrupting men;" "it must be the art of enlightening them and making them better."

[64] "The legislator is in command of the future. He must make men what he wants them to be."

faire triompher des vues universelles" (698).[65] Crocker has commented on this preference for the universal over the individual. An obsessive pursuit of justice, he writes, can contradictorily become unjust because it leads to "an abstract love of humanity allied with contempt of individual men" (194). The Jacobins effectively individualized citizens, but when they did so, they viewed them with contempt. The Revolution's leaders celebrated and praised the "people" yet at the same time they were hostile towards individuals. "Le peuple," Robespierre remarked, "vaut toujours mieux que les individus" (5: 209).[66] While failing to find worth in the individual, Robespierre held the people in high esteem.

The notion that the people is worth more than the individual is similarly expressed by Rousseau. Crocker remarks that Rousseau warned against showing pity towards individuals. He summarizes Rousseau's ideas: "The more abstract our love of mankind is, the more virtuous it becomes. If we are not careful to 'generalize' pity and 'extend it over all mankind,' it will degenerate into the weakness of pitying unworthy individuals" (144). Robespierre and Saint-Just undoubtedly held this view as well. They preferred to express an abstract compassion for the people and for humanity. If they ever expressed pity and sympathy, it was only towards those whom they had determined to be innocent and virtuous; they were resolute in defending persecuted virtue. At a Jacobin Club meeting, Robespierre reminded them that the revolutionaries had to stand guard and protect the pure and innocent patriots: "Nous sommes résolus de défendre de tout notre pouvoir la vertu persécutée. . . . La première des vertus républicaines est de veiller pour l'innocence" (10: 490).[67] To extend pity or compassion towards supposed enemies of liberty would be "to sacrifice the people for the sake of one individual" (Blum, *Rousseau* 178). Robespierre sharply rejected any suggestion that clemency be granted towards a

---

[65] "You must decide not what matters to an individual, but what matters to the Republic; you must not yield to private views, but must make universal views triumph."

[66] "The people . . . is worth more than individuals."

[67] "We are resolved to defend persecuted virtue with all our power . . . . The first of all republican virtues is to stand guard for innocence."

declared enemy, but championed mercy being granted towards all of humanity. He argued, "Indulgence pour les royalists, s'écrient certaines gens. Grâce pour les scélérats! Non: grâce pour l'innocence, grâce pour les faibles, grâce pour les malheureux, *grâce pour l'humanité!*" (emphasis added; 10: 357).[68] Apparently, the villains had been dismissed by Robespierre from the body of humanity. They did not figure into his vision of a people that is pure and full of goodness. Rather, individuals whom he recognized as standing apart from the mass of the people were not only evil, they were condemned as non-members of humanity.

This way of thinking inevitably led to the designation of the enemy as an un-human being. Individuals who were not considered part of the mass of the people were dehumanized both in language and in perception. Schama disputes the claim that verbal violence was merely rhetorical, and contends that there was a connection between the cries for the brutal death of enemies and the actual shedding of blood. Both the rhetoric and actions resulted in "the complete dehumanization of those who became victims" (Schama 860). By denying the victims an individual human identity, the accusers and executioners were able to carry out the elimination – physical or verbal – of the enemy without feeling the guilt associated with the killing of a fellow member of the human race. Throughout the Revolution, enemies were referred to as "*scélérats*," "*traîtres*," and "*calomniateurs*," among other terms. Robespierre added the word "*monstres*" to this list. "Ce sont les monstres que nous avons accusés," he repeated several times in one speech (10: 547).[69] Thus, in a sense, having used the identity of the individual to single out an enemy of the Revolution, the accusers then chose to de-personalize the accused by withdrawing his or her individual identity.

There was a distinct dichotomy between the reality of *le peuple* and Robespierre's ideal concept of it. His definition of the people was in fact a very

---

[68] "Indulgence for the royalists, some people cry out. Mercy for the scoundrels! No – mercy for innocence, mercy for the weak, mercy for the unfortunate, mercy for humanity!" (*ORFR* 375).
[69] "It is the monsters whom we have accused."

narrow one that encompassed only pristine, virtuous citizens, uncorrupted by personal interest. It was not constituted of any particular individuals; specific human beings did not in their collective sum create "the people." Consequently, he assigned to the abstract people the traits and values that he was unable to confirm in individual human beings. He said, "The morality which has disappeared in most individuals can be found only in the mass of people and in the general interest" (qtd. in Blum 160). Individuals proved to be a disappointment to Robespierre. He found that individuals exhibited weaknesses of character which he thought were contrary to humanity, and which he therefore attributed to conspiracy and corruption (Palmer 178). Yet his understanding of the people was faulty as well. Palmer speaks of Robespierre's "tragic misconception" of the people:

> The French people was nothing like what Robespierre imagined. It was not all compact of goodness; it was not peculiarly governable by reason; it was not even a unitary thing at all, for only a minority was even republican. Robespierre's "people" was the people of his mind's eye, the people as it was to be when felicity was established. (277)

Revolution had thus created such an abstract notion of the people that the characteristics attributed to it were impossible to verify empirically. No particular individuals fit the description of "the people," although it was the individual, not the people, who was recognized as a concrete, tangible being. The revolutionaries were forced to come to terms with this realization. As individuals failed to meet the strict criteria of the virtuous people, the Revolution became progressively radicalized. The revolutionaries continued to push for an elusive goal: they aimed for a republic of virtue in a nation where few if any individuals were deemed truly virtuous.

Chapter Four

The Female Individual and the French Revolution

La liberté civile et politique est,
pour ainsi dire, inutile aux femmes.
Prudhomme (1791)

The difficulty in reconciling the notion of the ideal citizen with the reality of individuals' political practice was never so apparent as in the case of the female citizen. Revolutionary principles expressed in the *Déclaration des droits de l'homme et du citoyen* promised certain universal rights to all citizens, but these principles soon were contradicted by the implementation of such rights. Freedom to express one's opinions, for example, as provided in the tenth and eleventh articles of the *Déclaration des droits* was soon revealed to have a limited meaning – a limitation which was based on the gender of the speaker. Olympe de Gouges, among others, brought to the fore the failure of the Revolution's leaders to grant these rights to women. In her own version of the *Déclaration des droits,* which she titled, *La déclaration des droits de la femme et de la citoyenne,* she unknowingly signaled her own fate when she asserted, "La femme a le droit de monter sur l'échafaud; elle doit avoir également celui de monter à la Tribune."[1, 2] The failure of the revolutionaries

---

[1] *Les Femmes dans la Révolution Française,* document 36, page 9. Each document has separate pagination. Henceforth, this source will be abbreviated *FRF,* followed by the document number and the page number.

[2] "Woman has the right to mount the scaffold; she must equally have the right to mount the rostrum" (*WRP* 91). English translations taken from this source, *Women in Revolutionary Paris 1789-1795. Selected Documents Translated with Notes and Commentary,* will henceforth be referenced with the abbreviation *WRP.*

to identify and correct this contradiction resulted in a clash between many women's expectations for universal human rights and the denial of those rights. The Revolution was committed to principles of equality – an ideal based on a universal, abstract, rights-bearing individual – however, this individual was quickly identified as a gendered, male human subject (Scott, French 2). Not only were women refused the rights of citizenship that were accorded to men, they were frequently cast into the groups of individuals who were considered to be outside of the unified people. Similar to the monarchists, scoundrels, enemies, and counterrevolutionaries who were eliminated from the republic both rhetorically and physically, women too were excluded from the unified nation of citizens. The exclusion of women from the public political sphere was based not so much on the contents of their speech and actions, but on their very physical nature – their femaleness. If individual men were excluded, it was because their words and actions did not coincide with the general will as interpreted by those in power; women were excluded because of their gender.

The republic was thus a gendered republic in which the dream of the Jacobin revolutionaries was to promote a particularly masculine patriotic ideology. Saint-Just phrased this vision by stipulating that, "Notre but est de créer un ordre de choses . . . tel qu'une mâle énergie incline l'esprit de la nation vers la justice" (703).[3] The period from 1789 to 1794 was fraught with ambiguities regarding women, and this vision, as espoused by Saint-Just, steadily gained momentum from 1789 onwards. Gutwirth has argued that "The Revolution was not improving women's lot, but worsening it" from 1789 to 1792, "And yet the early Revolution had not been so entirely closed against women as it was to become" (*Twilight* 251). By the start of 1794, the complete exclusion of individual female citizens from the public political arena had been firmly established

---

[3] "Our goal is to create an order of things . . . such that a male energy leads the spirit of the nation towards justice."

The equivocal meaning of the word "man," or "*l'homme*," in the *Déclaration des droits de l'homme* (a lexical ambiguity that is not unique to the French language), lent itself to the lack of clarity in defining who exactly was endowed with natural rights. The dual meaning of "man" – humanity or a male individual – provided a key source for disagreement over the identity of the rights-bearing individual. When the authors of the *Déclaration des droits de l'homme* wrote in the first article, "Les hommes naissent et demeurent libres, et égaux en droits,"[4] did they intend to convey the idea that all individuals, both male and female, were born free and equal in rights? Many female revolutionaries, and a few male ones as well, believed that in fact, "man" was an ungendered individual. Or were the declaration's writers determined to declare these rights for male individuals only? This question was increasingly answered in the affirmative as the Revolution progressed. Or did the writers choose not to clarify the ambiguity of the expression, purposely leaving the difficult issue unresolved? Blum contends that the *Déclaration des droits* could easily have specified the status of woman, but instead, it "slipped around the question" (*Rousseau* 208). Consequently, "The history of the next four years," as Blum goes on to explain, "was marked by governmental efforts to apply the word 'man' as 'human' in some spheres. . . and 'male' in others, namely, those concerned with political, educational, and social rights" (208). The unsettled issue could thus be manipulated by revolutionary leaders to their advantage. Women were praised for participating in political activities that contributed to the revolutionary cause, such as the October 5, 1789 march to Versailles to force the royal family back to Paris. However, women were not included in legal definitions of political rights.

The promise of the universal individual

Although women were not granted full rights of citizenship, and were excluded from the voting process, the Revolution nevertheless seemed to promise

---

[4] "Men are born and remain free and equal in rights."

that the new society would in fact be open to women's political expression and participation. Principles of equality and of universal, natural rights were assumed by many to mean that they would be applied to female citizens as well. Politically active women identified themselves as members of the sovereign people, and they considered themselves *citoyennes* of the sovereign nation, with the same full rights and responsibilities as their male counterparts. Female participation thus flourished during the revolutionary period; women joined protests, signed petitions, attended club and section meetings, participated in revolutionary festivals, and even formed their own revolutionary clubs. Some clubs, such as the Cercle Social invited women to speak at meetings, and created female societies.

The enthusiasm for women's political activity was shared by men as well – most notably by Condorcet, who in 1790 argued in the article, "Sur l'admission des femmes au droit de cité," that natural rights were indeed universal to all human beings, both male and female. In this article, which Landes considers the revolutionary period's most developed protest for women's rights (*Women* 113), he openly attacked the omission of women from the rights of citizenship. He insisted on the legitimacy of the female individual in the political realm because of her membership in the human community. Probing the meaning of natural rights, he concluded that rights were bestowed upon all humans because of their capacity to reason: "Or, les droits des hommes résultent uniquement de ce qu'ils sont des êtres sensibles, susceptibles d'acquérir des idées morales, et de raisonner sur ces idées" (122).[5] Women, capable of reasoning, therefore have the same rights as men: "Ainsi les femmes ayant ces mêmes qualités, ont nécessairement des droits égaux" (122).[6] One cannot deny rights to women that are granted to men because to do so would be to deny that any individual of the human species had any natural rights: "Ou aucun

---

[5] "Now the rights of men result simply from the fact that they are sentient beings, capable of acquiring moral ideas and of reasoning concerning those ideas" (qtd. in Landes 114).

[6] "Women, having these same qualities, must necessarily possess equal rights" (114).

individu de l'espèce humaine n'a de véritables droits, ou tous ont les mêmes" (122).[7] No individual being, therefore, could be determined to have essential human qualities that differed from those of any other human being. The essence of the female individual is the same as that of the male. When one refuses to grant rights to specific individuals, one denies the overall basic principle of natural rights. Condorcet calls this a violation of the principle, and states, "celui qui vote contre le droit d'un autre, quels que soient sa religion, sa couleur ou son sexe, a dès lors abjuré les siens" (122).[8] He argued that since rights were universal, the application of such rights must be universal as well.

Condorcet also rejected the most common argument used to justify the exclusion of women: the allegation of natural differences. As we will see most particularly in 1793, those opposed to granting rights to women pointed to natural and biological differences as reasons for women's inability to function as equals of the social contract. They also pointed to the functional differences between men and women, namely, the duties and roles the respective genders play in the household. Condorcet disagreed with the claim that physical or functional differences could serve as the primary basis for rights. He asked, "Pourquoi des êtres exposés à des grosseses, et à des indispositions passagères, ne pourraient-ils exercer des droits dont on n'a jamais imaginé de priver les gens qui ont la goutte tous les hivers, et qui s'enrhument aisément?" (122).[9] Here he argued that women are no more susceptible to physical indispositions than men, and are therefore not more limited than men by the physical side of their being. Moreover, women's sense of justice, which he admitted follows her feelings rather than her conscience, is a result of social forces at play, rather than natural forces: "ce n'est pas la nature, c'est l'éducation" (125).[10]

---

[7] "Either no individual of the human species has any true rights, or all have the same" (114).

[8] " . . . he or she who votes against the rights of another, of whatever religion, colour, or sex, has thereby abjured his own" (qtd. in Landes 115).

[9] "Why shouldn't human beings who are subject to pregnancy and passing indispositions be able to exercise the rights that one has never imagined denying to those who have gout in winter or catch cold easily?"

[10] "It is not nature but education" (qtd. in Landes 115).

He accordingly exposed the weakness of the argument based on physical differences and concluded that these differences did not constitute "une différence naturelle, qui puisse légitimement fonder l'exclusion du droit" (129).[11]

Olympe de Gouges, like Condorcet, wished to expose the Revolution's assertion of universal rights as faulty because of its practice of denying these rights to women. She sought to free the *Déclaration des droits* from the ambiguous use of the word "man." Scott describes the importance of de Gouges' *Déclaration des droits de la femme*:

> It is arguably the most comprehensive call for women's rights in this period; it takes the Revolution's universalism at its word; and it exposes the incompleteness of that universalism in its own paradoxical attempts to represent women as abstract individuals by calling attention to the differences they embody. (*Only* 20)

By substituting "man and woman," and at times only "woman," for the word "man" in the *Déclaration,* de Gouges effectively exposed the inconsistency in the Revolution's promise of universal rights, since women were clearly not enjoying the freedoms and equality that were declared in 1789. Like Condorcet, de Gouges refused to accentuate the differences between the sexes, and, as Godineau observes, she chose instead to emphasize what the two sexes had in common: reason, and consequently, rights (*Citoyennes* 271). De Gouges wrote that French legislators will ask of women, "Femmes, qu'y a-t-il de commun entre vous et nous?", to which women will need to reply, "Tout" (*FRF* 36: 12).[12] Thus, the reasoning capacity is an all-inclusive argument for claims to rights; no other attributes are of significance or consequence.[13] What she protested against was man's wish to rule over woman as a despot, in spite of the fact that women are a "un sexe qui a reçu toutes les facultés

---

[11] ". . . a natural difference that could legitimately provide the basis for the exclusion of rights."

[12] "Women, what is there in common between you and us? Everything" (*WRP* 92).

[13] She did not, however, completely ignore the physical differences between the sexes. For example, she hailed women as courageous "in maternal suffering" ["dans les souffrances maternelles" (*FRF* 36: 7)].

intellectuelles" (*FRF* 36: 6).[14]   Downplaying the physical differences, both de Gouges and Condorcet chose to separate biology and political identity (Scott, *Only* 48). There was never a dispute over men's claims as individuals, but de Gouges had to demand that women be considered as individuals as well in order for them to be a member of the aggregate of individuals that form the general will. Scott sums up de Gouges' arguments by explaining that "De Gouges argued for women's inclusion in politics on the grounds of their individuality" (32). The drive for women's equality therefore had to be based on the struggle to be recognized as concrete individuals.

The Cercle Social, whose members would be included in the Gironde faction, was one club that was actively advocated the cause for women in 1790 and 1791. Among its members were Condorcet, Madame Roland, and Etta Palm d'Aelders, all of whom proposed changes that would improve women's legal status. Not only did it welcome women as regular members, it was the first to do so; it encouraged a woman – Etta Palm – to deliver a speech before its political club, the Confédération des Amis de la Vérité; and it created an exclusively female section to further the rights of women (Kates 163, 172-73). Kates praises the Cercle Social as "one of the most important centers where an embryonic campaign for women's rights was launched during the early years of the French Revolution" (164). One Cercle Social publication, "Du sort actuel des femmes," expressed the imperative need to speak out concerning the exclusion of women from the exercise of rights. The writer demanded,

> Mais est-il permis de garder le silence quand, après avoir décrété les droits de l'homme, on a entendu ceux qui ont concouru à cette oeuvre, dire, avec ostentation, que les droits de la femme n'étoient

---

[14] "A sex which is in full possession of its intellectual faculties" (*WRP* 89).

> rien, et ne pouvant être autre chose que les bêtes de somme de
> l'humanité? (*FRF* 35: 11)[15]

This publication argued for an interpretation of the *Déclaration des droits de l'homme* according to a universal application of rights and harshly criticized those who subscribed to the declaration's principles, only to refuse those principles to women. "La moitié de l'espèce humaine est privée de ses droits naturels," it contended (*FRF* 35: 1).[16] The Cercle Social was thus determined to put women's rights on its agenda.

The Cercle Social in particular fought for legislation that would be fair and just towards women regarding marriage and divorce laws, as well as inheritance law. In a petition addressed to the National Assembly, it criticized divorce laws that favored the husband, and called for the establishment of divorce laws that would create a more equitable division of properties. Moreover, the freedom to divorce was inherently connected to a woman's natural right to freedom (Kates 167). Kates explains, "a liberal divorce law was seen as a prerequisite for developing women into dignified citizens. . . . Female political equality first required wives to become free and independent" (167). In taking up divorce law as an issue of primary importance, the members of the Cercle Social were in effect acting on their belief that because the rights-bearing individual was an abstract, genderless being, women were necessarily accorded rights as well. Therefore, these rights needed to be asserted and applied to French female citizens. They recognized the daily concerns of French women, and saw that women's lives did not demonstrate that the principles of the rights of man and citizen were being universally applied. Rather than arguing exclusively for an abstract inclusion of women's voices into the general will, the Cercle Social also argued for specific legislation that would be more favorable to women.

---

[15] "But is it permitted to keep silent when, after having decreed the rights of man, we have heard those who helped bring about this declaration say, with ostentation, that the rights of women are nothing, since they are nothing other than beasts of burden for humanity?"

[16] "Half of the human species is deprived of their natural rights."

Etta Palm d'Aelders articulated these concerns in numerous speeches where her two principal criticisms attacked unequal educational opportunities for girls, and inequality between spouses under marriage and divorce laws. Addressing the National Assembly, she implored the legislators not to discriminate against women with unjust laws. Her speech began with an appeal to equal rights for all individuals and for laws that would reflect these rights:

> La philosophie a tiré la vérité des ténèbres: l'heure sonne: la justice, soeur de la liberté, appelle à l'égalité des droits tous les individus, sans différence de sexe, les lois d'un peuple libre doivent être égales à tous les êtres, comme l'air et le soleil. . . . Trop long-tems enfin la tyrannie la plus odieuse étoit consacrée par des lois absurdes. (*FRF* 33: 38)[17]

These absurd laws, as she termed them, did not provide for the equality that should be granted to all individuals, including, of course, female individuals. Just as the air and the sun are universally accessible to all of humanity, so must liberty and equality. The foundation for her argument, like that of Condorcet, a fellow associate of the Cercle Social, was the abstract concept of universal rights. However, the remainder of her address did not continue along this vein of purely abstract reasoning; rather, she used the theoretical base to justify her subsequent demands for practical reforms. She protested in particular an article in the code of civil order which stipulated that the charge of adultery could be pursued only by the husband; a woman convicted of this offense would receive one to two years in prison (Levy, Applewhite, Johnson *Women,* 76). Discriminatory laws such as this, she claimed, were a form of tyranny against women. In fact, she and other female activists believed that a society that did not grant natural rights to each member could not claim to be free but was tyrannical (Godineau, "Autour" 101). To rectify this injustice, Palm proposed specific reforms,

---

[17] "Philosophy has drawn truth from the darkness; the time has come; justice, sister of liberty, calls all individuals to the equality of rights, without discrimination of sex; the laws of a free people must be equal for all beings, like the air and the sun . . . . For too long, the most odious tyranny was consecrated by absurd laws" (*WRP* 75-76).

chief among them, that the wife be recognized as an equal partner in marriage. She argued, "Les pouvoirs de l'époux et de l'épouse doivent être égaux et individuels. Les lois ne peuvent établir aucune différence entre ces deux autorités; elles doivent protection égale" (*FRF* 33: 39).[18] Both the man and the woman in marriage were to be acknowledged as individuals and treated with equal protection under the law.

Legislation regarding education, marriage and divorce were not the activist women's only specific demands for equality. Many women also claimed that the right to bear arms applied equally to men and to women. Théroigne de Méricourt, and two leaders of the Club des Citoyennes Républicaines Révolutionnaires, Pauline Léon, and Claire Lacombe, actively pursued the right to bear arms. In a petition presented to the National Assembly dated March 6, 1791, Pauline Léon and about 300 signatories vigorously asserted that women had the right to bear arms. They sought this right in order to defend themselves, and in true revolutionary fashion, to defend the *patrie* as well. The petition began, "Législateurs: Des femmes patriotes se présentent devant vous, pour réclamer le droit qu'a tout individu de pourvoir à la défense de la vie & de la liberté" (*FRF* 31: 1).[19] They unmistakably intended "tout individu" to be taken literally, in its most universal meaning. They in effect called on the legislators to define rights-bearing individuals as not only male, but also as female. Appealing to universal rights accorded by nature, they pointed out that the *Déclaration des droits* had in fact acknowledged this universal right when, in article two, it granted the right to resistance to oppression (Applewhite and Levy, Women and Radicalization 89). "Vous ne pouvez nous refuser, & la société ne peut nous ôter ce droit que la nature nous donne," they admonished the legislators, "à moins que l'on ne prétende que la Déclaration des Droits n'a point d'application pour les femmes, & qu'elles doivent se laisser égorger comme des agneaux, sans avoir le droit

---

[18] "The powers of husband and wife must be equal and separate. The laws cannot establish any difference between these two authorities; they must give equal protection" (*WRP* 76).

[19] "Legislators : Patriotic women come before you to claim the right which any individual has to defend his life and liberty" (*WRP* 72).

de se défendre" (*FRF* 31: 2).[20] These strongly worded demands were not, as Cerati commented, "une simple adresse. C'est un manifeste où l'égalité des droits est réclamée pour tous les humains" (43).[21] This sort of manifesto was more than a call for equal rights, it was also a call to action. It specifically requested that women obtain permission to acquire arms, to practice maneuvers with them, and to be placed under the command of the former French Guard (*FRF* 31: 4). By claiming this right, these women were fundamentally asserting the right to take an active part in public life (Cerati 43). They wanted heed the call of the Revolution and to defend the it against the schemes of its enemies.

Shortly after Léon presented her petition, Théroigne de Méricourt delivered a speech at the Société Fraternelle des Minimes, where she too pressed for the right to bear arms so that women could effectively stand guard against counterrevolutionary intrigues. She described her goal of organizing a female army corps whose purpose was twofold: to exercise equal rights, and to do so in order to dismantle the plots of counterrevolutionary activity and save the *patrie en danger*. She warned, "Des scélérats foudroyés ont un plan de division . . . afin de préparer des partis qui seront toujours funestes à la liberté, si votre vigilance ne déjoue les trames criminelles ourdies par nos ennemis" (*FRF* 40: 2).[22] The solution she offered was the opportunity to exercise their natural right to bear arms: "Armons-nous; nous en avons le droit par la nature & même par la loi" (*FRF* 40: 3).[23] By doing so, women would engage in public political involvement and would break the chains of injustice that men had placed on them:

---

[20] "You cannot refuse us, and society cannot deny the right nature gives us unless you pretend the Declaration of Rights does not apply to women, and that they should let their throats be cut like lambs, without the right to defend themselves" (*WRP* 73).

[21] " . . . simple address. It is a manifesto where equality of rights is claimed for all humans."

[22] "Some nasty villains have a plan for division . . . to prepare those who will always be enemies of liberty, if your vigilance does not foil the plots hatched by our enemies."

[23] "Let us arm; nature and even law give us the right to do so" (qtd. in Gutwirth, Twilight 326).

> Montrons aux hommes que nous ne leur sommes inférieures ni en
> vertus, ni en courage. . . . Françoises, je vous le répète encore,
> élevons-nous à la hauteur de nos destinées; brisons nos fers; il est
> temps enfin que les Femmes sortent de leur honteuse nullité, où
> l'ignorance, l'orgueil, & l'injustice des hommes les tiennent asservies
> depuis si longtemps. (*FRF* 30: 3, 5)[24]

Rejecting any notion that women were less capable than men when it came to

fighting to preserve liberty, or less deserving of "a civic crown" or "une couronne

civique" (7), Méricourt exhorted women to demonstrate their strength as free

individuals and to refuse the inferior status that unjust, ignorant men had forced upon

them.

The drive for women to be included in the exercise of natural rights kept pace

with the revolutionary zeal that motivated men to participate in the political body.

Just as male revolutionaries insisted that each individual was obligated to contribute

to the good of the whole, female revolutionaries searched for an equal opportunity

to fulfill this obligation. The president of the Dijon women's club, Blandin

Demoulin, remarked,

> Comme dans ce gouvernement chaque individu forme partie
> intégrante du tout, il doit donc coopérer en ce qui le concerne au bien
> de la république; il s'ensuit nécessairement que les femmes, qui font
> partie de la société, doivent contribuer, autant qu'elles le peuvent, au
> bien de tous. (*Révolutions* 189: 367)[25]

This female activist undeniably saw herself as an integral part of the whole. She

considered herself an individual who was one of the building blocks of society and

a member of the body politic. She believed that her duty as such an individual was

---

[24] "Let us show men that we are not inferior to them, either in virtue or in courage. . . . Women of France, I say it again, let us rise up to the heights of our destinies; let us break the chains; it is finally time that women leave behind their shameful worthlessness where the ignorance, pride and injustice of men enslaved them for so long."

[25] "Since in this government each individual is an integral part of the whole, each individual must therefore work towards the good of the republic; it follows that women, who are part of the society, must contribute as much as they can to the good of all."

precisely to serve the republic in the same manner that all male individuals were called upon to do. After all, she asked, "que peuvent faire tous les individus isolés l'un de l'autre?" (*Révolutions* 189: 367).[26]

The Club des Citoyennes Républicaines Révolutionnaires[27], created in May 1793, also declared that one of its primary purposes was precisely to contribute to the good of the republic. This militant and controversial women's organization, under the leadership of Claire Lacombe and Pauline Léon, became active in revolutionary politics in the summer of 1793. In its formal registration with the authorities of the Commune of Paris, the society defined its mission in terms that were commonly used and familiar in revolutionary rhetoric.: "Cette société a pour but de délibérer sur les moyens de déjouer les projets des ennemis de la république" (*Moniteur* 16: 362).[28] In orations and printed material, revolutionary patriots were called upon to *déjouer les projets des ennemis*, and in their stated goals, this club made the indentical claim. The printed regulations for these *républicaines révolutionnaires* expounded on their registered objective. In the preamble to their regulations, they listed their duties as *citoyennes* in the newly created organization: "To learn well the Constitution and laws of the Republic, to attend to public affairs, to succor suffering humanity, and to defend all human beings who become victims of any arbitrary acts" (qtd. in Levy, Applewhite and Johnson 161). The club's stated overall purpose was thus not confined to women's unique interests; rather, it declared the same purpose that male revolutionary leaders, clubs, and factions had proclaimed as well.

If "women's issues" had been defined by domestic concerns such as the availability of foodstuffs, inflation, and hoarding, the club would not have fit the description of a club with "women's issues" as its *raison d'être*.[29] Landes puts it

---

[26] "What can individuals do if they are isolated one from another?"

[27] The Club des Citoyennes Républicaines Révolutionaires will be referred to as Club des Citoyennes henceforth.

[28] "This society has as its goal to deliberate on ways to thwart the plans of the enemies of the republic."

[29] Hufton maintains that the Club des Citoyennes was created to combat the subsistence crisis, particularly hoarding and inflation; see *Women and the Limits of Citizenship*, 25. Several other critics, such as Godineau and Landes, disagree. See Godineau, *Citoyennes Tricoteuses*, 159-160; and Landes,

candidly when she writes, "Women's issues were not foremost on its agenda" (141).
And Cerati describes their project by pointing to their indefatigable zeal and activity
for the Revolution: "Inlassables, elles réclamaient des mesures concrètes qui les
situaient à la pointe du combat révolutionnaire" (190).[30] In short, these women – de
Gouges, Léon, Méricourt, Palm, Lacombe, the members of the Club des Citoyennes,
as well as countless others – were fighting to be recognized as veritable citizens and
members of the sovereign body. While they were not granted full rights of
citizenship, they nevertheless identified themselves as individual citizens of a
sovereign nation.

Citoyen/Citoyenne

Women's claims to citizenship were complicated by the varying views of
what exactly constituted citizenship. There is, in fact, much debate in current
research over how one might accurately define citizenship. If one were to define
citizenship by the exercise of one's political rights, the ability to vote and to be voted
into public office, as Paule-Marie Duhet defines it (165), then the revolutionary
women clearly did not possess citizenship. If, on the other hand, we point to political
activity and evidence of politicization of individuals as expressions of citizenship,
then revolutionary women were practicing citizenship. Levy and Applewhite support
this view of citizenship. They contend in their article, "Women and Militant
Citizenship," that when women participated in grass-roots democratic institutions,
marched in ceremonies, participated in revolutionary *journées*, mobilized support,
and exercised surveillance, "they identified themselves as members of the sovereign
body politic – *citoyennes* notwithstanding their exclusion from codified political

---

Women and the Public Sphere, 140-42.
[30] "Indefatigable, they demanded concrete measures that placed them at the forefront of the
revolutionary struggle."

rights of citizenship" (97).[31] In another article, these writers acknowledge the difficulty in reconciling the two different concepts of citizenship. They observe that a constitutionally legislated notion of the citizen is incompatible with the concrete activities that demonstrate a claim to sovereignty. They write, "Constitutional legislation legitimized an abstract nation of passive citizens, who embodied a sovereignty that it in no way acted upon," (Women, Democracy 68). However, they also point out that, "singularly aware and active Parisians, men and women, were claiming sovereignty by practicing an almost daily intervention in public affairs" (68). Therefore, while the debate will continue over what constitutes citizenship – whether it is women's actions or their constitutional status – women were undoubtedly yearning to participate fully in the sovereign body.

The constitution of 1791 made a distinction between "active" and "passive" citizens and designated women as the latter.[32] In this constitution active citizens were defined as men over age 25 who met certain tax and professional qualifications; their tax payment had to equal three days' work, and they could not be domestic servants. All others were labeled passive citizens – a category that included domestic servants, less wealthy and propertied men, and women. Active citizens possessed full political rights of citizenship, such as the right to vote and to bear arms, whereas passive citizens did not enjoy the same full rights of citizenship. In other words, some citizens were more equal than others. Although Camille Desmoulins and a minority in the Assembly argued that active citizens ought to be defined by their political activity, the majority opinion determined that political action did not in fact establish citizenship (Scott, *Only* 35). In June 1793, the new constitution reconsidered the notion of the active citizen and expanded it to include formerly passive male citizens,

---

[31] The French language makes a distinction between a male citizen (*citoyen*) and female citizen (*citoyenne*) – a distinction that does not exist in English. The French terms will be used here to uphold that distinction.

[32] For some discussions on citizenship, see Landes 121-122; Rudé 134; Scott, *Only Paradoxes* 34-35; Applewhite and Levy's article, "Women and Democracy;" Godineau, *Citoyennes* 112, 122; Scott's article, "French Feminists and the Rights of 'Man'."

and erased the previous distinction between active and passive citizens. Women, who had been relegated to the status of passive citizenship in 1791, were left out of the revised definition of the citizen in 1793 completely. Godineau describes this omission as a "situation nouvelle qui rend l'injustice plus criante" (122).[33] In addition, the deputies placed women into the same category that counterrevolutionary male individuals were pushed into – that of the foreigner or outsider. A publication by the Cercle Social decried this gesture. It protested against a penal code that contained the same punishment for women as for foreigners: "Vous avez assimilé les femmes et les filles françoises aux hommes étrangers à la patrie. Quoi! les femmes ne seroient pas citoyennes!" (*FRF* 35: 12).[34]

While the constitution of June 1793 formally eliminated the category of passive citizenship, the notion of the passive citizen – a member of the nation but not possessing political rights – continued to surface in revolutionary thought. Women were referred to as *citoyennes* by male revolutionaries, even though women were not explicitly identified as full citizens with rights of citizenship. However, the Revolution's speakers and writers were not necessarily united in their use of the terms. The term *citoyenne* turns out to be quite nuanced, complex, and full of contradictions. Godineau poses the important question, "Qu'est-ce donc qu'une *citoyenne* qui ne possède pas les droits politiques du citoyen?" (Autour 92).[35] Godineau has offered very useful insights into the term *citoyenne* that shed light on some of the complexities of its use in revolutionary writings and speeches. In "Autour du mot *citoyenne*," she traces its diverse uses and meanings as they appeared in both Enlightenment and revolutionary discourse. After surveying writings such as those of Diderot, Rousseau and dictionaries of the time, she finds that the terms *citoyen* and *citoyenne* were used inconsistently. A *citoyenne* frequently referred to

---

[33] " . . . a new situation that makes the injustice even more glaring."
[34] "You have likened French women and girls to foreign men. What then! Women would not be citizens!"
[35] "What, then, is a *citoyenne* who does not possess the political rights of a citizen?"

a female inhabitant, or to a female member of a household that was headed by a *citoyen*. A man was considered to be a *citoyen* on the basis of possession of political rights, however, rather than on his role in a household. This confusion, Godineau writes, is carried into the Revolution:

> Le double sens du mot, que révèlent dictionnaires et écrivains, et qui est en quelque sorte à l'origine de cet imbroglio, sera fondamental dans l'usage qui en sera fait pendant la Révolution: les femmes sont citoyennes comme habitantes . . . bien qu'elles ne soient 'pas vraiment' citoyennes puisque ne possédant pas de droits politiques. (Autour 93)[36]

Revolutionary use of the term complicated the issue further by suggesting that not all women earned the title *citoyenne*. Even if it was a given that *citoyennes* did not possess political rights, appropriate patriotic activity was required in order for a woman to deserve the title. Godineau refers to *citoyenne* as a "titre qui se mérite" (Autour 94).[37] Women were thus caught in a double bind: first of all, they were excluded from what was to become a narrow definition of citizenship that was restricted to male citizens with political rights. Secondly, while an exclusively female type of citizenship was implied, some individual women were subsequently excluded from this body of citizens as well. In other words, no woman was a *citoyen*, and some women were not even *citoyennes*.

This rhetorical prohibition of women from citizenship is evident in Citizen Chabot's address to Claire Lacombe. He referred to her in the following manner, "Madame Lacombe, car je ne peus pas la traiter de Citoyenne. . . ." (*FRF* 50: 2).[38] Accusing her and the Club des Citoyennes of intrigue and counterrevolutionary activity (among his complaints were that they dared attack Robespierre and called

---

[36] "The double meaning of the word, as seen in dictionaries and other writings, and is in some way at the origin of this imbroglio, will be fundamental in how it will be used during the Revolution: women are *citoyennes* in the sense of inhabitants . . . although they are 'not really' citizens because they do not possess political rights."

[37] " . . . a title that is earned."

[38] "Madame Lacombe – I just can't consider her a citoyenne" (*WRP* 187).

him *Monsieur* Robespierre), he refused to address her as *citoyenne* because to do so would be to elevate her to a higher status, of which he believed she was undeserving. As Godineau explains, "La citoyenne est la femme qui mérite de la Nation et de la Révolution" (Autour 97).[39] An editor of *Révolutions de Paris*, Prudhomme also withheld the title of *citoyenne* from the women in the Club des Citoyennes and sharply criticized women's public political activity. Women's actions which he deemed positive were those of *citoyennes,* whereas women's political societies, towards which he was hostile, were referred to as only "clubs de femmes" (Godineau, Autour 95-96). As we will shortly see in more detail, Prudhomme and many other revolutionaries believed that a woman's contribution to the *patrie* was her private, domestic virtue, not a public virtue. Fulfilling her domestic duties granted a woman the title *citoyenne,* according to Prudhomme. Ironically, as Godineau observes, for Prudhomme the title *citoyenne* thus referred to a non-political woman (Autour 97). Prudhomme, in criticizing the women's club in Lyon, wrote, "Nous conjurons les bonnes citoyennes de Lyon de rester chez elles, de veiller à leur ménage" (*Révolutions* 185: 235).[40] On the other hand, according to female revolutionaries, the title *citoyenne* denoted a political woman. But because male revolutionaries attributed the *citoyenne* to the private, domestic sphere only, she could not be regarded as her own political individual.

The denial of the female rights-bearing individual

Prudhomme was certainly not alone in rebuking women's public political actions. As revolutionary leaders were faced with the increasing involvement of women in political affairs the definition of the virtuous individual became increasingly narrow as well. If Robespierre and the Jacobin leaders had insisted on the virtuous individual as the true foundation of the general will, the identity of this

---

[39] "The citoyenne is a woman who has earned the recognition of the nation and the Revolution."
[40] "We implore the good *citoyennes* of Lyon to stay home to look after their households" (qtd. in Blum, Rousseau 209).

individual and of this virtue was restricted to a solely masculine being. Female virtue was defined in different terms entirely, and by the end of 1793, women were shunned from the public political sphere, and consequently, from exercising a public political virtue.

Abstract ideas about women and nature provided the rhetorical basis for the drive to exclude women from the public sphere. Condorcet had referred to reason and nature in his essay on women's right to vote, and other revolutionary leaders would do the same. The vast majority of them would not reach the same conclusions as had Condorcet, however. Nature could be a liberating force by providing the source for freedoms and rights of the individual in society, but nature could also be a limiting force, as in the case of women. Nature imposed physiological and biological limits on women that rendered them unfit for the political domain, and appropriate only for domestic, familial activity. Ignoring the enthusiastic political activity of countless individual women, the male leaders chose to disregard concrete proof that women were fully capable of exercising political rights, and had the intellectual capacity to understand and appreciate justice, liberty, and devotion to the *patrie*. They reverted to considerations of nature to justify their contempt towards women's attempts to assert themselves politically.

Enlightenment thought certainly held sway concerning theories of the proper, and supposedly natural, role for women in society.[41] Revolutionary leaders followed the Enlightenment tradition of considering the female individual according to nature. When the *philosophes'* specifically discussed women and nature, they often referred to a concept of nature that stressed the physiological distinctions between men and women. Bloch and Bloch describe how, according to the traditional Enlightenment view, women were in many ways closer to nature than men because of their physiological role in sex and motherhood (32). It would follow that because of this

---

[41] See Paul Hoffmann's *La Femme dans la pensée des lumières* and Samia I. Spencer's edited volume, *French Women and the Age of Enlightenment*, for a more thorough treatment of the topic of women in the Enlightenment.

closeness, women were more bound by natural, biological constraints than men, and their actions more likely to be determined by nature.

Diderot spelled out how women were entirely controlled by their physiological composition in his article "Sur les femmes." He described woman as a being that is thoroughly subject to the commands of her uterus and to a particularly female mental lapse, which he called "le délire hystérique" (952). Badinter explains that according to Diderot, the uterus is a woman's essence, and determines her thought and experience (34). Hysteria causes a woman to have incomprehensible emotional swings that mark her inferiority. He called woman, "un être extrême dans sa force et dans sa faiblesse" (949). Not only does the uterus function as the determinant in her emotional and intellectual capabilities, it also serves to establish woman in the societal role as procreators (Bloch and Bloch 38). In the Tahitian society that Diderot describes in *Supplément au voyage de Bougainville*, the sexual freedom "is the source of a genuinely free existence for the male Tahitians," but for women, it is not a liberating freedom (Bloch and Bloch 38). It is instead a functional freedom that facilitates reproduction, and as a result, firmly situates woman into the role of sexual object and mother.

Rousseau's description of Sophie in book five of *Emile* was also based on his understanding of the natural and biological functions of women. The woman's maternal duties were to raise children, please her husband, remain chaste and stay at home. This role, Rousseau thought, was justified by the physical differences between the sexes. And these physical differences, he wrote, "doivent influer sur le moral" (*Emile* 431).[42] He goes on to argue that as a consequence, men are active and strong, and women are passive and weak; women are made specifically to please men and to be subjected to them. This, he states, is not the law of love, but the law "de la nature" (*Emile* 431). To act in any way that is contrary to the law of nature regarding the sexes would be misguided, so he discourages this. He advises, "Voulez-vous

---

[42] " . . . must have their moral effect" (260).

toujours être bien guidé, suivez toujours les indications de la nature. Tout ce qui caractérise le sexe doit être respecté comme établi par elle" (*Emile* 438).[43]

While Diderot and Rousseau referred to nature to support their views on the role of women in society in these cited examples, they used abstract women as their models. Diderot's Tahitian women and Rousseau's Sophie were certainly imagined characters. They represented no specific individual woman in particular, but these women were intended to represent women in general nevertheless. Revolutionary leaders used much the same argumentation when they disputed women's freedom to exercise political rights. They too referred to nature, and they too spoke in general terms about women. Had they spoken only of the individual political women whose actions they were trying to suppress, they would have been forced to come to grips with the contradictions between their revolutionary principles of natural rights and their political practice of denying women these rights. The Jacobin leadership would not have been able to justify its eventual repression of women's political associations. Claude Bazire, for one, annoyed when a fellow deputy ventured to point out this contradiction in principles, retorted, "Qu'on ne me parle plus de principes" (*Moniteur* 18: 300).[44]

As women's organizations became increasingly active in 1793 – particularly the Club des Citoyennes – the issue of women's political involvement came to the fore. Several notable speeches, writings, and debates focused on the role of women in the revolutionary society in that year. The invocation of nature to assign women a maternal and domestic role was repeatedly used by public figures who sought to restrict women to the private sphere. Politically active women were thought to be unnatural; their activity was deemed inappropriate because it was contrary to their natural function. Hérault de Séchelles' speech at the Festival of Unity (August 10, 1793) was also a clear example of the tendency to resort to nature when the question

---

[43] "Would you always be well guided? Always follow the indications of Nature. All that characterizes [the] sex[es] ought to be respected or established by her" (261).

[44] "Let no one say anything more to me about principles" (*WRP* 217).

of women's role came up. His discourse echoed Diderot's statements on woman's physiological function and, hence, social function. He implored women to give birth to the future heros and combatants against tyranny: "O femmes! la liberté attaquée par tous les tyrans, pour être défendue a besoin d'un peuple de héros. C'est à vous à l'enfanter" (*Moniteur* 17: 367).[45] These heroes were presumed to be male. Woman's role was not to be heroic in the same fashion as men, but to facilitate, encourage and raise male children to perform heroic actions for the *patrie*. He reminded women of this imperative: "Que toutes les vertus guerrières et généreuses coulent avec le lait maternel dans le coeur des nourrissons de la France!" (*Moniteur* 17: 367).[46] Like the women in Diderot's Tahiti, French women were to serve the republic in a physiological manner, by making good use of their uterus to produce virtuous men.

Hérault also urged women to breast-feed their children, but this was hardly an original feature of his speech. The natural function of breast-feeding resurfaced time and again in speeches, writings, and visual representations of women, and was undoubtedly reminiscent of Rousseau who had advocated a return to maternal breast-feeding in *Emile*. He criticized upper class mothers in France who were neglecting this natural duty, and believed that the deprivation of the mothers' breast milk resulted in personal and social evil (Gutwirth, *Twilight* 61). The return to maternal breast-feeding would also lead to societal reform, Rousseau suggested. At a meeting of the Commune of Paris, Pierre-Gaspard , the *procureur général* of the Commune, mentioned breast-feeding as well when he spoke of the laws of nature. He believed that a woman's contribution to the republic was determined by her physical traits, which included her mammary glands. Refusing the idea that women could exercise the same rights as men, he asked, "Est-ce aux hommes que la nature a confié les

---

[45] "O women! Liberty is attacked by tyrants, and to be defended, needs a heroic people. It is up to you to give birth to them."
[46] "May all the warlike and generous virtues flow with a mother's milk into the hearts of the children of France!"

soins domestiques? nous a-t-elle donné des mamelles pour allaiter nos enfants?" (*Moniteur* 18: 450).[47]

Prudhomme also invoked natural differences in order to condemn women's political clubs. In 1791, around the same time that Condorcet was using nature to argue for universal rights, Prudhomme was using nature to deny those same rights. He declared that nature prescribed different functions for the sexes, and that this natural order must not be violated: "Mais la nature, à laquelle la société ne doit déroger que malgré elle, a prescrit à chacun des sexes ses fonctions respectives" (*Révolutions* 83: 230).[48] He added that a women's functions were to serve society as good mothers, to please their husbands, and to nourish and take care of their children. While he explained that nature had dictated separate roles, he added that women would not be able to exercise civil and political liberties in any case. They did not have that intangible quality – "cette ardeur à qui tout cède"[49] – which led men to heroic actions in the name of the *patrie*. Therefore, "La liberté civile et politique est, pour ainsi dire, inutile aux femmes et par conséquent doit leur être étrangère" (*Révolutions* 83: 230-31).[50] Thus he rejected the notion that nature universally granted rights to all individuals. He went even further to say that not only did nature withhold these political and civil rights from women, women would not have any use for these rights in the first place. Such rights would be entirely inconsequential for women.

In other issues of his journal, Prudhomme elaborated that not only should women be preoccupied with strictly domestic matters, they should not even attempt to become fully politically educated, beyond what they would need to teach proper virtues to their children. In his brief journalistic debate with Blandin Demoulin in

---

[47] "Is it to men that nature confided domestic cares? Has she given us breasts to breast-feed our children?" (*WRP* 219).

[48] "But nature, whose wishes society must not depart from, has prescribed to each of the sexes their respective functions."

[49] "That fervor to which everything yields."

[50] "Civil and political liberty are, so to speak, useless to women, and consequently must be alien to them" (qtd. in Gutwirth, *Twilight* 286).

1793 over the legitimacy of women's clubs, he called women's political clubs the scourge of good domestic virtues. The gist of his criticism was that these clubs gave women a political awareness that he thought was inappropriate for good mothers. While he approved of women gathering to discuss their duties, he wanted them to do so only informally, with their children on their laps, and certainly without a regular meeting time with minutes taken (*Révolutions* 185: 234). Moreover, their political education was to be quite limited. Women should not even have "la prétention d'entendre le contrat social à livre ouvert" (*Révolutions* 185: 235).[51] And recalling Rousseau's Sophie and Julie, he pointed out that Julie never took her children to a political club meeting, and that Emile never permitted Sophie to attend a political society either (*Révolutions* 189: 371). His adamant refusal to allow women the opportunity to become politicized indicated that he perceived an element of danger associated with politically active women.

Underlying many of the arguments against women's political activism and claims to equal rights was the inherent fear that politicized women out in the public were dangerous to the public order. Women who remained in the private sphere would not be able to provoke public disturbances which could threaten the Revolution. When women did express their concerns, their expressions were perceived, as Gutwirth comments, as disruptive outbursts, no matter what the content (*Twilight* 285). She explains,

> The sheer inability to cope with these manifestations by women, to integrate them conceptually or practically into ongoing policies, demonstrates the inability of political men . . . to contemplate what the advent of a republic and its rhetoric of freedom might augur for women. (*Twilight* 284)

Men's inability to cope with these so-called outbursts was effectively demonstrated in the latter half of 1793.

---

[51] " . . . the pretentiousness to listen to a reading of the social contract."

The Club des Citoyennes became involved in an often violent debate with market women from Les Halles over the wearing of the cockade, or *cocarde,* and the red phrygian cap, or *bonnet rouge*, both revolutionary symbols. Antagonism between these two groups of women over the cockade and phrygian cap (and other underlying issues as well), resulted in physical fights and altercations between the two groups of women. The reactions of the police and of the Convention over these disputes revealed the extent to which they blamed the disorder on women's claims to universal rights. In fact, many of the police reports on the disturbances did not address only the specific controversy of the cockade and the women fighting over it, but attributed the broader issue of women's rights as the fundamental cause for the disturbances. One police report cited the women who demanded compulsory wearing of the cockade as evildoers and criticized the fact that they "inspirent aux femmes le désir de partager les droits politiques des hommes" (Caron 154).[52] Another officer wrote in his report, "Ces ennemis de la tranquillité publique flattent l'amour-propre des femmes, cherchent à leur persuader qu'elles ont autant de droits que les hommes au gouvernement de leur pays" (Caron 165).[53] The cockade issue thus brought to the fore the question of universal rights and whether or not individual women shared in the rights that men had been granted.

In debating the cockade and phrygian cap disputes, the Convention was faced with two matters to consider. The first was the tangible proof that many individual women were demonstrating a strong sense of public civism and political awareness. The second was the intangible notion of nature, and the question of knowing whether nature accorded women the same universal rights as men or had established constraints on women's exercise of rights. When the Convention was compelled to grapple with these two issues, the debate was actually quite brief. In fact, there was scarcely a debate or discussion, other than short comments by Fabre d'Eglantine,

---

[52] " . . . inspire in women the desire to share the political rights of men."
[53] "These enemies of public tranquility flatter women's self-esteem, [and] seek to persuade them that they have as many rights to the government of their country as men."

Chaumette, and Charles Charlier, and a report by André Amar. Godineau has pointed out that Amar's report was the only legislative text that raised the question of political rights for women (*Citoyennes* 176). Perhaps the lack of a sustained debate on political rights for women is as significant as the few comments that we do have. Considering that throughout the revolutionary period, women had been active in political events and had voiced their desire to partake fully in popular sovereignty, there was relatively little formal consideration of the issues. Amar's report and the brief comments that preceded and followed it provided the definitive legislative discussion and decision. The issue would hardly resurface afterwards in an official context.

At the end of October 1793 Fabre proposed that the Committee of General Security draw up a report on the women's revolutionary societies. He stated that this report was of particular urgency because the militant revolutionary women "sont actuellement dans la rue" (*AP* 78: 21).[54] He observed that the women who were involved in the public disputes were not taking care of their households and children. Instead, he reprehended them as "une sorte de chevaliers errants . . . qui se répandent partout et causent des troubles dans la ville" (*AP* 78: 21).[55] These women were shirking their domestic duties, and consequently, participating in counterrevolutionary activity. He warned his fellow deputies that these women's activities were, "encore un moyen de nos ennemis" (*AP* 78: 21).[56] His motion that the situation be studied closely was quickly adopted, and the following day, Amar issued his conclusive report on policies regarding women clubs.

Amar's speech on behalf of the Committee of General Security synthesized many of the arguments against women's rights and public political involvement that had been uttered over the previous few years. He addressed what he considered the two central issues regarding the disruptions over the cockade and red cap. Firstly, he

---

[54] " . . . are in the street at this moment."
[55] " . . . like errant knights . . . who are scattered about everywhere and cause troubles in the town."
[56] " . . . yet another method of our enemy."

asked whether women were capable of exercising political rights and of taking an active role in governmental affairs. To his own question, he answered negatively. Women, he claimed, had neither the moral nor physical strength to do so. "L'opinion universelle repousse cette idée" (*Moniteur* 18: 299).[57] This universal opinion to which he referred was not founded in any poll or thorough examination of attitudes, as Blum writes, but was "to be found by searching within the heart of the virtuous patriot who was in touch with nature" (*Rousseau*, 213). Amar believed that his own understanding of nature was sufficient enough to defend the exclusion of women from politics. Furthermore, he did not weigh the evidence of specific women who had demonstrated full intellectual and leadership capabilities. To do so would have perhaps forced him to reverse his decision.

Amar's second question concerned women's political associations, and he asked, "Peuvent-elles délibérer réunies en associations politiques ou Sociétés populaires?" (*Moniteur* 18: 299).[58] To this also, he answered no. Again referring to what he believed were the dictates of nature, he replied that women were called to domestic, private duties, and to behave otherwise would be to sacrifice the natural calling and to upset the social order, "car la nature . . . a posé ces limites" (*Moniteur* 18: 299).[59] He went on to describe the proper, natural woman as a wife and mother who raises her children to understand public virtues and elevate their souls in liberty, and encourages her husband to love the *patrie*. We have already seen that Robespierre defined morality and virtue by one's love for the nation and its laws. But here, women were called on to be virtuous in a different way. They were destined to encourage others, presumably males, to be virtuous. Amar stated, "La femme est naturellement destinée à faire aimer la vertu" (*Moniteur* 18: 300).[60] Female virtue was thus not the same as male virtue.

---

[57] "Universal opinion rejects this idea" (*WRP* 215).
[58] "Can they deliberate together in political associations or popular societies?" (*WRP* 215).
[59] ". . . because nature... imposed these limits" (*WRP* 215).
[60] "Woman is naturally destined to make virtue loved" (*WRP* 216).

After Amar finished reading his report, one lone voice objected, and then the decree to ban women's popular societies was adopted. Charlier, the lone dissenting voice, reminded Amar that women were, after all, part of the human species. The legislators had no right to deny reasoning, thinking human beings the right to assemble. "A moins que vous ne contestiez que les femmes font partie du genre humain, pouvez-vous leur ôter ce droit commun à tout être pensant?" (*Moniteur* 18: 300).[61] The right to assemble, he maintained, was a universal right, and could not be denied unless the associations were upsetting public order or breaking the law; and even then, he claimed, they would be pursued through legal means. Charlier based his objection on his understanding that all human beings were endowed with the capacity to reason, as Condorcet had similarly concluded a few years before him. This intangible quality, he believed, was distributed equally to men and women alike. His view of nature was thus quite different from that of Amar. Charlier saw nature as a liberating force that accorded natural rights to all individuals, regardless of the physical differences between the sexes.

Charlier's line of reasoning was quickly silenced by Bazire, however. Being forced to confront the logic of Charlier's argument, Bazire resorted to another line of reasoning. He switched the focus of the discussion from Charlier's abstract concept of woman as a member of the human species to woman as a tangible actor in the public arena. He attempted to summarize Amar's remarks by saying, "Il est donc uniquement question de savoir si les Sociétés des femmes sont dangereuses. L'expérience a prouvé, ces jours passés, combien elles sont funestes à la tranquillité publique" (*Moniteur* 18: 300).[62] Yet Amar's report did not necessarily address this question. Amar did not base his opinion solely on the disruption of public order, but on the more general concept of women's natural rights and duties. Bazire perhaps

---

[61] "Unless you are going to question whether women are part of the human species, can you take away from them this right which is common to every thinking being?" (*WRP* 217).

[62] "It is only a question of knowing whether women's societies are dangerous. Experience has shown these past days how deadly they are to the public peace" (*WRP* 217).

realized the inherent contradictions and weaknesses in Amar's argument when challenged by Charlier. In order to continue to deny women the right to assemble, Bazire would have to base his argument on a consideration of the concrete political activity of women's societies. He thus had the last word, and women's political societies were declared strictly forbidden.

The Revolution had not completely eliminated female figures from the public sphere, however. Although women were discouraged from active political participation, they were nevertheless important in a passive sense – the female body became an allegory for revolutionary ideals and appeared prominently in engravings, paintings, and other visual formats with a political purpose.[63] Women were encouraged to maintain only domestic, private virtues, but they nonetheless were quite visible and celebrated in public venues. These public women were not, however, specific individuals that were held up and praised for their revolutionary activity. Instead, they were anonymous, generic illustrations of female figures whose bodies were used to exalt revolutionary ideals. Female figures often represented liberty, equality, truth, the death of the aristocracy, and the victory of the republic. In fact, the first seal of the republic was the depiction of a woman in a Roman tunic (Landes, *Women* 159). Revolutionary leaders rebuffed the notion that real women were equal to the task of exercising liberty, but in these depictions, women appear to be capable of crushing tyranny singlehandedly. Moreover, she represents the complete embodiment of the entire body politic. This solitary, individual female is revered for representing the whole of popular sovereignty, while conversely, in practice, the individual female was expelled from the very practice of popular sovereignty. In other words, in allegorical representations, an individual woman could represent the whole, while in reality individual women were excluded from this whole. Addressing this issue, Lynn Hunt notes that, "Woman could be representative

---

[63] See Madelyn Gutwirth's exhaustive work on imagery, *Twilight of the Goddesses*, as well as research by Joan B. Landes, Lynn Hunt, Dorinda Outram, Anthony Vidler, Elizabeth Liris, and Mona Ozouf for discussions on allegorical representations, the female body, and female symbolism.

of abstract qualities and collective dreams because women were not about to vote or govern" (Political 39). Real women were thus banished to private, domestic life while their imaginary representations were elevated to public, symbolic roles and functions.

Revolutionary festivals revealed this paradox as well. The revolutionary period was filled with festivals celebrating fraternity, reason, unity, the fall of the monarchy, and the establishment of the republic, among others.[64] These carefully choreographed and planned fetes designated women as representing the domestic sphere or as fulfilling a merely symbolic role. For example, at the celebration of the cult of Reason in November 1793, women were assigned to play the symbolic part of Reason's goddesses (Gutwirth, *Twilight* 276). In provincial festivals of Reason as well, there was a female figure, often a statue, at the center of the festival. She embodied liberty, reason, or even victory (Ozouf 98-99). At the Festival of the Supreme Being in June of the following year, Jacques-Louis David scripted a representation in which real women were to portray female domestic virtues. He planned for the women to wear white, carry flowers, and promise to marry only citizens who have served the *patrie*; mothers were told to thank the Supreme Being for their fertility (Baker, *Old* 390). This display of republican women lucidly demonstrated how public women were forced to conform to what Schama terms the "Rousseauean-Jacobin doctrine of the wife-mother role for women patriots" (749). At civic festivals and in other visual formats, women were used to represent allegorically the Revolution's ideals which they were not, however, permitted to enjoy in reality. They also were called upon to demonstrate the particularly female virtues of domesticity that did not necessarily correspond with the ideals of liberty and equality. This paradox reveals the sharp differences between the abstract notions of universal rights and the demands made on real women.

---

[64] See Mona Ozouf's *La fête révolutionnaire* for a thorough discussion of festivals and celebrations.

Female individuality?

Female republican virtue was thus ultimately inconsistent with male virtue. The separation of functions within the republic along gender lines severed women from full participation in the expression of popular sovereignty. When women attempted to express their patriotic sentiments in the same way as men – by forming societies, and speaking publicly, for example – they were accused of violating the principles of nature that prescribed gender-based roles. In November 1793, Chaumette refused to allow a delegation of women to speak at one meeting and from assembling in further meetings as well because such activities would lead them to deny their natural being as women. A woman who wanted the same rights and privileges as a man was, in his eyes, a woman who wanted to be a man. She was not viewed as a woman who wanted to exercise her universal, individual rights, but as one who wanted to act as a man. He criticized these women by saying, "Il est affreux, il est contraire à toutes les lois de la nature qu'une femme se veuille faire homme" (*Moniteur* 18: 450).[65] Women who chose to make a public political statement were abandoning their natural household and maternal duties, and could not be permitted to do so. Nature, he said, told man to be a man, and told woman to be a woman: "Au nom de cette même nature, restez ce que vous êtes" (*Moniteur* 18: 450).[66] Just two years after Olympe de Gouges claimed universal rights for women, and just months after the Club des Citoyennes formally declared their participation in frustrating the plots of the republic's enemies, Chaumette had summed up the Revolution's ultimate reply to women's demands for equality.

> Eh! depuis quand est-il permis d'abjurer son sexe? depuis quand est-il décent de voir des femmes abandonner les soins *pieux* de leur ménage, le berceau de leurs enfants, pour venir sur les places

---

[65] "It is horrible, it is contrary to all the laws of nature for a woman to want to make herself a man" (*WRP* 219).
[66] "In the name of this very nature, remain what you are" (*WRP* 220).

publiques, dans les tribunes aux harangues, à la barre du sénat?
(*Moniteur* 18: 450)[67]

Any attempts to make the term "man" synonymous with "human being" would finally be met with dismissal. As a result, women were excluded from the political body.

Women's individuality was glossed over in the name of an abstract nature that imposed a physiological function on women. The Revolution's leaders feared and mistrusted individual women's concrete political activity for to recognize this activity would have forced them to reconsider their view of women. To accept women's ability to partake in the social contract would be to recognize them as individuals who were integral participants in the social contract. Gutwirth writes that the speeches and images of the Revolution "left little space for the emergence of female individuality that could lead to women's equality or parity with men" (Rights 165). Female individuality had to be rejected if women were to be excluded from the public political sphere.

One deputy to the Convention had in fact suggested the term "individual" be used instead of the equivocal term "man," in order to champion the equality of rights. Pierre Guyomar, explained in April 1793 that, "Si j'ai employé le mot *individu,* c'est qu'il m'a paru le plus propre à indiquer les hommes de tout sexe, de tout âge, tous membres, à mon avis, de la grande famille qui habite le monde" (*FRF* 45: 2).[68] He went on to attack the exclusion of women from the full membership in the general will and insisted that because they were excluded from it, they were not subject to it. Here, he revealed the dilemma besetting a policy for reserving political rights for men only. He asks, "Où est donc l'obligation de la femme d'obéir à des lois auxquelles

---

[67] "Well! Since when is it permitted to give up one's sex ? Since when is it decent to see women abandoning the pious cares of their households, the cribs of their children, to come to public places, to harangues in the galleries, at the bar of the senate?" (*WRP* 219).

[68] "If I used the word individual, it is because it seemed the most appropriate to indicate [people] of all genders, of all ages, all members, in my opinion, of the large family that inhabits the world."

elle ne concourt ni directement ni indirectement?" (*FRF* 45: 4).[69] The contradiction arising from a refusal to grant women equal rights was untenable, and Guyomar answered his own question by concluding, "Je soutiens que la moitié des individus d'une société n'a pas le droit de priver l'autre moitié du droit impresciptible d'émettre son voeu" (*FRF* 45: 4).[70] The Revolution's governments and constitutions protected the inalienable rights of male individuals only. As Landes puts it, "Only male rights to full individuality were protected" (*Women* 158). Guyomar evidently understood that this was a debilitating deficiency in a society that professed liberty and equality.

But there were few other male revolutionaries who arrived at the same conclusions as Guyomar. Ultimately, *les droits de l'homme* were not *les droits de la femme*. In excluding women from the body politic and from the exercise of citizens' rights, the male revolutionary leaders were in effect denying women's individuality and humanity. If the theoretical basis of popular sovereignty under the social contract was the rights-bearing individual, and women were denied these rights, then women were not considered to be individuals in the same sense as men. Furthermore, it was determined that men had natural and inalienable rights simply due to their existence as human beings. When women were excluded from the rights outlined in the *Déclaration des droits de l'homme,* they were relegated to a status of human being that was different than that of men. Definitive speeches by men such as Chaumette and Amar revealed that they perceived women as a different type of human being. Charlier argued that women must not be denied rights unless their inclusion in the *genre humain* was contested. Charlier's protest proved accurate. Women were denied rights, and this denial did, in fact, imply that women were of a different *genre* of human being than men.

---

[69] "Where, then, is a woman's obligation to obey laws that she did help bring about either directly or indirectly?"

[70] "I maintain that half of the individuals in a society does not have the right to deprive the other half of the inalienable right to express their wishes?"

Conclusion

The philosophical journey from classical thought of the eighteenth century to modern thought of the nineteenth century was characterized by what Foucault calls the appearance of "man." As Foucault describes it, the human subject was missing in classical thought, but man finally emerged as both a subject that knows and an object of knowledge. He refers to Velázquez' painting *Las Meninas* to illustrate this point. He is not interested in what the painting represents, however, but in how it serves as a model for representation (Dubreuil-Blondin 121). *Las Meninas* presents an interminable reciprocity between the spectator and the characters in the space of the canvas. The *infanta* and the characters surrounding her are looking out towards us while we look at them, and the painter is looking towards us as well, as he clutches his palette and paintbrush, ready to paint another stroke onto his canvas. But his canvas is turned away from us, and we are unable to see what he is painting. Foucault writes that this invisible canvas "empêche que soit jamais repérable ni définitivement établi le rapport des regards" (*Mots* 21).[1] The characters are looking out of their canvas space towards what is not fixed; they are gazing into the emptiness that is before them, and into the space that we occupy but is invisible to them. The painting, according to Foucault, is a representation of classical representation. He describes this representation as follows: "Elle entreprend en effet de s'y représenter en tous ses éléments, avec ses images, les regards auxquels elle s'offre, les visages qu'elle rend visibles, les gestes qui la font naître" (*Mots* 31).[2] What is missing here, and in classical thought, however, is the subject. Within this

---

[1] ". . . it prevents the relation of these gazes from ever being discoverable or definitely established" (5).
[2] "And, indeed, representation undertakes to represent itself here in all its elements, with its images, the eyes to which it is offered, the faces it makes visible, the gestures that call it into being" (16).

ensemble, we find an emptiness: "la disparition nécessaire de ce qui la fonde, – de celui à qui elle ressemble et de celui aux yeux de qui elle n'est que ressemblance. Ce sujet même – qui est le même – a été élidé" (*Mots* 31).[3] Before the end of the eighteenth century, Foucault writes, *man* did not exist: "l'*homme* n'existait pas" (*Mots* 319).

The *philosophes* analyzed the individual human beings as a member of the human species, and human knowledge as it is represented by sense perception and memory, for example. The eighteenth-century philosophers defined individuals in a manner that was rational, that privileged mechanisms, and that supposed a general order in nature. Foucault points out that this type of analysis characterized classical thought and reassured the thinkers that their knowledge was legitimate. At the turn of the eighteenth century the invisible space faced by *las meninas* was finally filled. Foucault explains that this emptiness was filled by the appearance of man: "L'homme apparaît avec sa position ambiguë d'objet pour un savoir et de sujet qui connaît: souverain soumis, spectateur regardé" (*Mots* 323).[4] Modern thought emerged when human knowledge about human beings became self-referential.

During the French revolutionary period, classical representations of the individual were no longer sufficient or reliable for the establishment of the new political power. Hypothetical states of nature, universal movement, or the laws of matter were inadequate in determining the individual's place in the new political system. Abstract ideas of social contracts, citizenship, and sovereignty demanded practical considerations and practical implementations of political ideals. Thus, the concrete existence of individuals – both male and female – came to the fore.

But along with the appearance of the concrete individual came difficult consequences. Those in political power during the Revolution were soon confronted

---

[3] ". . . the necessary disappearance of that which is its foundation – of the person it resembles and the person in whose eyes it is only a resemblance. This very subject – which is the same – has been elided" (16).
[4] "Man appears in his ambiguous position as an object of knowledge and as a subject that knows: enslaved sovereign, observed spectator" (312).

with the difficulty of reconciling their abstract theories about human beings with their concrete experience with individual human beings. Robespierre and Saint-Just in particular discovered that individuals did not necessarily fit their idea of the virtuous citizen who loved the nation and its laws. As we saw previously, this contradiction resulted in a sharp distrust of individuals. Consequently, many individuals lost their lives at the guillotine, or lost their liberties through mechanisms such as the Law of 22 Prairial. The contradictions between the abstract individual and the concrete individual had negative consequences for the female individual as well. The male political leaders rejected women's claims that they, too, were rights-bearing individuals on whom the social contract was based. The revolutionary period eventually solidified the denial of equal rights for individual women.

The French Revolution, situated at the end of the eighteenth century, was a turning point for the individual human being. Classical thought's abstractions were beginning to disappear and modern thought's reliance on the individual's concrete existence was beginning to emerge. The Revolution was situated within this change in knowledge strategies. The concept of the individual during the Revolution was thus clearly caught at the crossroads between classical and modern thought.

Bibliography

Primary Sources

Eighteenth-Century Writings and Documents

Archives parlementaires de 1787 à 1860. First series. (1787 to 1799). Eds. M. J. Mavidal and M. E. Laurent. 82 vols. Paris: Dupont, 1879-1913.

Caron, Pierre, ed. *Paris pendant la terreur: rapports des agents secrets du ministre de l'intérieur.* Vol. 1. Paris: Librairie Alphonse Picard, 1910.

Condillac, Etienne Bonnot, Abbé de. "Traité des sensations." *Oeuvres complètes de Condillac.* Vol. 4. Paris: 1803.

Condorcet, Marie-Jean-Antoine-Nicolas Caritat, marquis de. "Sur l'admission des femmes au droit de cité." *Oeuvres de Condorcet.* Vol. 10. Paris, 1847. 121-30.

Danton, Georges-Jacques. *Oeuvres de Danton.* Ed. A. Vermorel. Paris: 1867.

Desmoulins, Camille. *Oeuvres de Camille Desmoulins.* Ed. M. Jules Clarentie. 2 vols. Paris: Charpentier, 1906.

Diderot, Denis. "Autorité politique." *Oeuvres complètes.* Vol. 5. 537-44.

_____. "Droit naturel." *Oeuvres complètes.* Vol. 7. 24-29.

_____. *Observations sur le Nakaz. Oeuvres politiques.* Ed. Paul Vernière. Paris: Garnier, 1963.

_____. *Oeuvres.* Paris: Editions Gallimard, 1951.

_____. *Oeuvres complètes.* Paris: Hermann, 1981.

_____. *Réflexions sur le livre* De l'esprit *par M. Helvétius. Oeuvres complètes.* Vol. 9. 303-12.

_____. *Le Rêve de d'Alembert. Oeuvres.* 886-934.

_____. *Supplément au voyage de Bougainville. Oeuvres.* 963-1002.

_____. *Sur les femmes. Oeuvres.* 949-958.

Duvergier, Jean B., ed. *Collection des lois, décrets, ordonnances, réglemens, avis du conseil d'état de 1788 à 1830.* Vol. 5. Paris: Société du Recueil Sirey, 1831-1949.

Les Femmes dans la Révolution Française. Vol. 2. Paris: EDHIS, 1982.

Helvétius, Claude-Adrien. *De l'esprit.* Paris: Editions Sociales, 1959.

Hemsterhuis, François. *Lettre sur l'homme et ses rapports* avec le commentaire inédit de Diderot. Ed. Georges May. New Haven: Yale UP, 1964.

Holbach, Paul-Henri Thiry, baron d'. *Système de la nature.* Vol. 1. Hildesheim: Georg Olms Verlag, 1966.

_____. *Système social.* Vol. 1-3. Hildesheim: Georg Olms Verlag, 1966.

La Mettrie, Julien Offray de. *L'Homme-machine. Oeuvres philosophiques.* Vol. 1-2. Hildesheim: Georg Olms Verlag, 1970.

Marat, Jean-Paul. *Oeuvres politiques: 1789-1793.* Eds. Jacques DeCock and Charlotte Goetz. 10 vols. Brussels: Pôle Nord, 1995.

Markov, Walter and Albert Soboul. *Die Sansculotten von Paris: Dokumente zur geschichte der Volksbewegung 1793-1794.* Berlin: Akademie Verlag, 1957.

Montesquieu, Charles-Louis de Secondat, Baron de. *De l'esprit des lois. Oeuvres complètes.* Paris: Seuil, 1964. 528-795.

_____. *Lettres persanes. Oeuvres complètes.* Paris: Seuil, 1964. 63-151.

Morelly, M. *Code de la nature ou le véritable esprit de ses lois.* Ed. Gilbert Chinard. Paris: R. Clavreuil, 1950.

_____. *Le Prince.* 1751.

Réimpression de l'ancien Moniteur. 32 vols. Paris: 1858-1863.

Révolutions de Paris. Paris: 1791.

Robespierre, Maximilien. *Oeuvres de Maximilien Robespierre.* 10 vols. Paris: Société des Etudes Robespierristes, 1930-1967.

Rousseau, Jean-Jacques. *Du contrat social.* Ed. Pierre Burgelin. Paris: Flammarion, 1992.

_____. *Discours sur l'économie politique. Oeuvres complètes.* Vol. 3. Paris: Gallimard, 1964. 240-78.

_____. *Discours sur l'origine et les fondements de l'inégalité parmi les hommes.* Ed. Jacques Roger. Paris: Flammarion, 1992.

_____. *Emile.* Paris: Garnier, n. d.

_____. *Essai sur l'origine des langues. Oeuvres complètes.* Vol. 5. Paris: Gallimard, 1959. 370-408.

_____. *Julie ou la Nouvelle Héloïse.* Ed. Michel Launay. Paris: Flammarion, 1967.

Saint-Just, Louis-Antoine. *Oeuvres complètes de Saint-Just.* Ed. Michèle Duval. Paris: Editions Gérard Lebovici, 1984.

Sieyès, Emmanuel. *Qu'est-ce que le tiers état?* Ed. Roberto Zapperi. Geneva: Droz, 1970.

Thomas, Antoine-Léonard. *Essai sur le caractère, les moeurs et l'esprit des femmes dans les différens siècles.* 1772. Ed. Badinter. 49-162.

English Translations of Eighteenth-Century French Writings and Documents

Baker, Keith Michael, ed. *The Old Regime and the French Revolution.* University of Chicago Readings in Western Civilization. Vol. 7. Chicago: U of Chicago Press, 1987.

Diderot, Denis. *Rameau's Nephew and D'Alembert's Dream.* Trans. Leonard Tancock. Harmondsworth: Penguin, 1966.

_____. *Political Writings.* Trans. John Hope Mason and Robert Wokler. Cambridge: Cambridge UP, 1992.

Helvétius, Claude-Adrian. *De l'Esprit; or, Essays on the Mind.* Sterling, VA: Thoemmes Press, 2000.

Holbach, Paul-Henri Thiry, baron d'. *The System of Nature.* Vol. I. NY: Garland Publishing, 1984.

La Mettrie, Julien Offray de. *Man a Machine and Man a Plant.* Trans. Richard A. Watson and Maya Rybalka. Indianapolis: Hackett Publishing Company, 1994.

Levy, Darline Gay, Harriet B. Applewhite, Mary Durham Johnson, eds. *Women in Revolutionary Paris 1789-1795: Selected Documents Translated with Notes and Commentary.* Urbana: U of Illinois P, 1980.

Montesquieu, Charles-Louis de Secondat, Baron de. *The Persian Letters.* Trans. George R. Hardy. Indianapolis: The Bobbs-Merril Company, 1964.

_____. *The Spirit of the Laws.* Trans. Anne M. Cohler. NY: Cambridge UP, 1989.

Rousseau, Jean-Jacques. *Discourse on Political Economy and the Social Contract.* Trans. Christopher Betts. NY: Oxford UP, 1999.

_____. *Emile.* Trans. William H. Payne. NY: Prometheus Books, 2003.

_____. *Julie or the New Heloise.* Trans. Philip Stewart and Jean Vaché. Hanover: UP of New England, 1997.

_____. *On the Origin of Language.* Trans. John H. Moran. Chicago: U of Chicago P, 1986.

_____. *The Social Contract and the Discourses. A Discourse on Political Economy.* Trans. G.D.H. Cole. NY: Alfred A. Knopf, 1993.

Stephens, H. Morse. *The Principal Speeches of the Statesmen and Orators of the French Revolution.* Vol. 2. Oxford: Clarendon Press, 1892.

Stewart, John Hall, ed. *A Documentary Survey of the French Revolution.* New York: Macmillan, 1951.

Walzer, Michael. *Regicide and Revolution: Speeches at the Trial of Louis XVI.* Ed. and Introduction by Walzer. Trans. Marian Rothstein. Cambridge: Cambridge UP, 1974.

Secondary Sources

Applewhite, Harriet B. and Darline Gay Levy. Introduction. *Women and Politics.* 1-21.

_____, eds. *Women and Politics in the Age of the Democratic Revolution.* Ann Arbor: U of Michigan P, 1990.

_____. "Women, Democracy and Revolution in Paris, 1789-94." Spencer 64-79.

_____. "Women, Radicalization, and the Fall of the French   Monarchy." Applewhite and Levy, *Women and Politics* 81-107.

Badinter, Elisabeth. Preface. *Qu'est-ce qu'une femme?: un débat.* Ed. Badinter. Paris: P. O. L., 1989. 7-48.

Baker, Keith Michael. "A Foucauldian French Revolution?" *Foucault and the Writing of History.* Goldstein. 186-205.

_____. *Inventing the French Revolution: Essays on French Political Culture in the Eighteenth Century.* Cambridge: Cambridge UP, 1990.

_____, ed. *The Old Regime and the French Revolution.*   University of Chicago Readings in Western Civilization. Vol. 7.   Chicago: U of Chicago Press, 1987.

_____. "Sovereignty." *A Critical Dictionary of the French Revolution.* Eds. François Furet and Mona Ozouf. Trans. Arthur Goldhammer. Cambridge, Mass.: Belknap Press of Harvard UP, 1989.

Barny, Roger. *Les Contradictions de l'idéologie révolutionnaire des droits de l'homme (1789-1796): droits naturels et histoire.* Paris: Diffusion les Belles lettres, 1993.

Bates, David W. *Enlightenment Aberrations: Error and Revolution in France.* Ithaca: Cornell UP, 2002.

Baum, John Alan. *Montesquieu and Social Theory.* Oxford: Pergamon Press, 1979.

Benasayag, Miguel. *Le mythe de l'individu.* Trans. Anne Weinfeld. Paris: Editions La Découverte, 2004.

Benrekassa, Georges. *La Politique et sa mémoire: la politique et l'historique dans la pensée des lumières.* Paris: Payot, 1983.

Besse, Guy. Introduction. *De l'esprit.* By Helvétius. 7-64.

Bloch, Maurice and Jean H. Bloch. "Women and the Dialectics of Nature in Eighteenth-Century French Thought." *Nature, Culture, and Gender.* Eds. Carol P. MacCormack and Marilyn Strathern. Cambridge: Cambridge UP, 1980. 25-41.

Blum, Carol. "Representing the Body Politic: Fictions of the State." Heffernan 123-34.

_____. *Rousseau and the Republic of Virtue: The Language of Politics in the French Revolution.* Ithaca: Cornell UP, 1986.

Bouloiseau, Marc. *La République jacobine.* Paris: Seuil, 1972.

Brooks, Peter. "The Revolutionary Body." Fort 35-54.

Brunetti, Franz. "De la loi naturelle à la loi civile." *Europe: Revue littéraire mensuelle* 661 (1984): 42-50.

Burchell, Graham. "Peculiar Interests: Civil Society and Governing 'The System of Natural Liberty'." Burchell, Gordon and Miller 119-51.

Burchell, Graham, Colin Gordon and Peter Miller, eds. *The Foucault Effect: Studies in Governmentality.* Chicago: U of Chicago P, 1991.

Cassirer, Ernst. *The Philosophy of the Enlightenment.* Trans. Fritz C. A. Koelln and James P. Pettegrove. Boston: Princeton UP, 1951.

Censer, Jack R. "Robespierre the Journalist." *Studies on Voltaire and the Eighteenth Century* 287 (1991): 189-96.

Cerati, Marie. *Le Club des Citoyennes Républicaines Révolutionnaires.* Paris: Editions sociales, 1966.

Chartier, Roger. "The Chimera of the Origin: Archaeology, Cultural History, and the French Revolution." Goldstein 167-86.

_____. *Les Origines culturelles de la Révolution française.* Paris: Seuil, 1990.

Chinard, Gilbert. Introduction. *Code de la nature.* By Morelly. 7-147.

Chisick, Harvey. Introduction. *Studies on Voltaire and the Eighteenth Century* 287 (1991). 1-16.

Crocker, Lester. *Jean-Jacques Rousseau: The Prophetic Voice (1758-1778).* New York: Macmillan, 1973.

Darnton, Robert and Daniel Roche, eds. *Revolution in Print: The Press in France 1775-1800.* Berkeley: U California P, 1989.

Derathé, Robert. *Jean-Jacques Rousseau et la science politique de son temps.* Paris: J. Vrin, 1970.

Desan, Suzanne. "Women's Experience of the French Revolution: An Historical Overview." Montfort 19-30.

Didier, Béatrice. *Ecrire la Révolution 1789-99.* Paris: P. U. F., 1989.

_____. *Histoire de la littérature française du XVIIIe siècle.* Paris: Nathan, 1992.

Driver, C. H. "Morelly and Mably." *Social and Political Ideas of Some Great French Thinkers.* Ed. F. J. C. Hearnshaw. London: G. G. Harrap, 1930. 217-52.

Dubreuil-Blondin, Nicole. "Le Philosophe chez Vélazquez: l'instrusion de Michel Foucault dans la fortune critique des *Ménines.*" *Revue d'Art Canadienne/Canadian Art Review* 20, 1-2 (1993): 116-29.

Duchet, Michèle. *Anthropologie et histoire au siècle des lumières.* Paris: A. Michel, 1995.

_____. "Diderot et 'l'Histoire des deux Indes': fragments pour une politique." *Europe: Revue Littéraire Mensuelle* 661 (1984): 51-57.

Duhet, Paule-Marie. *Les Femmes et la Révolution, 1789-1794.* Paris: Julliard, 1971.

Durkheim, Emile. *Montesquieu and Rousseau: Forerunners of Sociology.* Trans. Ralph Manheim. Ann Arbor: U of Michigan P, 1960.

Ehrard, Jean. *L'idée de nature en France dans la première moitité du XVIIIe siècle.* Paris: S.E.V.P.E.N., 1963.

Eisenstein, Elizabeth L. "The Tribune of the People: a New Species of Demagogue." *Studies on Voltaire and the Eighteenth Century* 287 (1991): 145-59.

Elyada, Ouzi. "Les récits de complot dans la presse populaire parisienne 1790-91." *Studies on Voltaire and the Eighteenth Century* 287 (1991): 281-92.

Fellows, Otis E. and Norman L. Torrey, eds. *The Age of the Enlightenment.* Englewood Cliffs: Prentice-Hall, 1971.

Fort, Bernadette, ed. *Fictions of the French Revolution.* Evanston: Northwestern UP, 1991.

Foucault, Michel. *Suveiller et punir: naissance de la prison.* Paris: Gallimard, 1975.

_____. *The Foucault Reader.* Ed. Paul Rabinow. New York: Pantheon, 1984.

_____. "Governmentality." Burchell, Gordon, and Miller. 87-104.

_____. *Les Mots et les choses: une archéologie des sciences humaines.* Paris: Gallimard, 1966.

_____. *The Order of Things: An Archaeology of the Human Sciences.* New York: Vintage Books, 1970.

_____. "The Political Technology of Individuals." Martin, Gutman, and Hutton. 145-162.

_____. "Politics and Reason." *Michel Foucault: Politics, Philosophy, Culture: Interviews and Other Writings, 1977-1984.* Ed. Lawrence D. Kritzman. New York: Routledge, 1988. 57-85.

_____. "Qu'est-ce que les Lumières?" *Dits et écrits.* Vol. 4. 679-688.

_____. "The Subject and Power." *Michel Foucault: Beyond Structuralism and Hermeneutics.* Eds. Hubert Dreyfus and Paul Rabinow. Chicago: U of Chicago P, 1982.

Frank, Francine Wattman and Paula A. Treichler. *Language, Gender, and Professional Writing Theoretical Approaches and Guidelines for Nonsexist Usage.* New York: Commission on the Status of Women in the Profession, Modern Language Association of America, 1989.

Furet, François. *Penser la Révolution française.* Paris: Gallimard, 1978.

Ganochaud, Collette. "Révolution et opinion publique chez Rousseau: autour des idéaux de liberté, égalité et de fraternité." *Studies on Voltaire and the 18th century* 324 (1994): 1-19.

Godineau, Dominique. "Autour du mot *citoyenne.*" *Mots* 16 (1988): 91-110.

_____. *Citoyennes tricoteuses: les femmes du peuple à Paris pendant la Révolution française.* Aix-en-Provence: Alinea, 1998.

Goldstein, Jan, ed. *Foucault and the Writing of History.* Oxford: Blackwell Ltd., 1994.

Goodman, Dena. "The Structure of Political Argument in Diderot's *Supplément au voyage de Bougainville.*" *Diderot Studies* 21 (1983): 123-37.

Gordon, Colin. "Governmental Rationality: An Introduction." Eds. Burchell, Gordon, and Miller. 1-51.

Gottheimer, Marjorie. "Diderot: The Emergence of a New Individualism." *Enlightenment Essays* 3 (1972): 126-34.

Goyard-Fabre, Simone. *Montesquieu: la nature, les lois, la liberté.* Paris: P. U. F., 1993.

Gutman, Huck. "Rousseau's *Confessions*: A Technology of the Self." Martin, Gutman, Hutton 99-121.

Gutwirth, Madelyn. "Citoyens, Citoyennes: Cultural Regression and the Subversion of Female Citizenship in the French Revolution." Waldinger 17-28.

_____. "The Rights and Wrongs of Woman: The Defeat of Feminist Rhetoric by Revolutionary Allegory." Heffernan 150-68.

_____. *The Twilight of the Goddesses: Women and Representation in the French Revolutionary Era.* New Brunswick: Rutgers UP, 1992.

Heffernan, James A. W., ed. *Representing the French Revolution: Literature, Historiography, and Art.* Hanover: UP of New England, 1992.

Hesse, Carla. *Publishing and Cultural Politics in Revolutionary Paris 1789-1810.* Berkeley: U Calif. Press, 1991.

Higonnet, Patrice. "Cultural Upheaval and Class Formation During the French Revolution." *The French Revolution and the Birth of Modernity.* Ed. Ferenc Fehér. Berkeley: U California P, 1990. 69-102.

_____. *Goodness Beyond Virtue: Jacobins During the French Revolution.* Cambridge: Harvard UP, 1998.

Hoffmann, Paul. *La Femme dans la pensée des lumières.* Paris: Editions Ophrys, 1977.

Horowitz, Irving Louis. *Claude Helvétius: Philosopher of Democracy and Enlightenment.* New York: Paine-Whitman, 1954.

Hudson, Nicholas. "Language, Abstract Thought and Political Power in Vico, Manderville, and Rousseau." *Studies on Voltaire and the Eighteenth Century* 303 (1992): 256-59.

Hufton, Olwen H. *Women and the Limits of Citizenship in the French Revolution.* Toronto: U of Toronto P, 1992.

Hunt, Lynn, ed. *Eroticism and the Body Politic.* Baltimore: Johns Hopkins UP, 1991.

_____. "Male Virtue and Republican Motherhood." *The French Revolution and the Creation of Modern Political Culture.* Ed. Keith Michael Baker. Vol. 4. Oxford; New York: Pergamon Press, 1994. 195-208.

_____. "The Many Bodies of Marie Antoinette: Political Pornography and the Problem of the Feminine in the French Revolution." Hunt, *Eroticism* 108-30.

_____. "The Political Psychology of Revolutionary Caricatures." *French Caricature and the French Revolution, 1789-1799.* Los Angeles: Grunwald Center for the Graphic Arts; Chicago: University of Chicago, 1988. 25-32.

_____. *Politics, Culture, and Class in the French Revolution.* Berkeley: U California Press, 1984.

Jacobus, Mary. "Incorruptible Milk: Breast-feeding and the French Revolution." Melzer 54-75.

Jaume, Lucien. *Le Discours jacobin et la démocratie.* Paris: Fayard, 1989.

Jourdain, Annie. "Le culte de Rousseau sous la Révolution: la statue et la panthéonisation du Citoyen de Genève." *Studies on Voltaire and the Eighteenth Century* 324 (1994): 57-77.

Kates, Gary. "'The Powers of Husband and Wife Must be Equal and Separate': The Cercle Social and the Rights of Women, 1790-91." Applewhite and Levy, *Women and Politics* 163-80.

Kaufmann, Jean-Claude. *Ego: Pour un sociologie de l'individu.* Paris: Nathan, 2001.

_____. *L'invention de soi. Une théorie de l'identité.* Paris: Hachette, 2004.

Kennedy, Emmet. *A Cultural History of the French Revolution.* New Haven: Yale UP, 1989.

Kleinbaum, Abby R. "Women in the Age of Light." *Becoming Visible: Women in European History.* Eds. Renate Bridenthal and Claudia Koontz. Boston: Houghton Mifflin, 1977. 217-35.

Kors, Alan Charles. *D'Holbach's Coterie: An Enlightenment in Paris.* Princeton: Princeton UP, 1976.

Kra, Pauline. "The Invisible Chain of the *Lettres Persanes.*" *Studies on Voltaire and the Eighteenth Century* 23 (1963): 7-60.

Landes, Joan B. "Representing the Body Politic: The Paradox of Gender in the Graphic Politics of the French Revolution." Melzer 15-37.

_____. *Visualizing the Nation: Gender, Representation and Revolution in Eighteenth-Century France.* Ithaca: Cornell UP, 2001.

_____. *Women and the Public Sphere in the Age of the French Revolution.* Ithaca: Cornell UP, 1988.

Launay, Michel. *Jean-Jacques Rousseau: écrivain politique.* Grenoble: ACER, 1971.

Lefebvre, Georges. *La Révolution française.* Paris: F. Alcan, 1930.

Lenardon, Dante. "The Genesis of Revolutionary Language and Vocabulary in the *Journal Encyclopédique.*" *Studies on Voltaire and the Eighteenth Century* 287 (1991): 311-17.

Levy, Darline Gay, and Harriet B. Applewhite. "Women and Militant Citizenship in Revolutionary Paris." Melzer 79-101.

Liris, Elizabeth. "La Révolution française à la recherche de son propre symbolisme." *Légende de la Révolution: actes du colloque international de Clermont-Ferrand.* June 1986. 161-71.

Martin, Luther H., Huck Gutman and Patrick H. Hutton, eds. *Technologies of the Self: A Seminar with Michel Foucault.* Amherst: U of Mass P, 1988.

Martin, Xavier. *Human Nature and the French Revolution from the Enlightenment to the Napoleonic Code.* Trans. Patrick Corcoran. NY: Berghahan Books, 2001.

Mas, Raymond. "La Nation: état de la question à la veille de 1789." *Légende de la Révolution: actes du colloque international de Clermont-Ferrand.* June 1986. 41-64.

Mason, John Hope and Robert Wokler, eds. and trans. Introduction. *Political Writings.* Denis Diderot. Cambridge: Cambridge UP, 1992.

Masters, Roger D. *The Political Philosophy of Rousseau.* Princeton: Princeton UP, 1968.

May, Gita. "Rousseau's 'Antifeminism' Reconsidered." Spencer 309-17.

McHoul, Alec and Wendy Grace. *A Foucault primer: Discourse, Power, and the Subject.* New York : New York UP, 1997.

Melzer, Sara E., and Leslie W. Rabine, eds. *Rebel Daughters: Women and the French Revolution.* New York: Oxford UP, 1992.

Merry, Henry J. *Montesquieu's System of Natural Government.* Lafayette: Purdue U Studies, 1970.

Miller, Stephen Paul. *The Seventies Now: Culture as Surveillance.* Durham: Duke UP, 1999.

Montfort, Catherine R. and J. J. Allison. Introduction. *Literate Women and the French Revolution of 1789.* Ed. Catherine R. Montfort. Birmingham: Summa, 1994. 3-17.

Mornet, Daniel. *Les origines intellectuelles de la Révolution française*. Paris: Colin, 1954.

Mortier, Roland. "Les Générations littéraires devant la Révolution française (1789-1792)." *Studies on Voltaire and the Eighteenth Century* 303 (1992): 17-30.

Naville, Pierre. *D'Holbach et la philosophie scientifique au XVIIIe siècle*. Paris: Gallimard, 1967.

Olivier, Paul. *Writing Your Thesis*. London: Sage Publications Limited, 2004.

O'Neal, John C. *The Authority of Experience: Sensationist Theory in the French Enlightenment*. University Park: Pennsylvania State UP, 1996.

Outram, Dorinda. "'Le Langage mâle de la vertu:' Women and the Discourse of the French Revolution." *The Social History of Language*. Eds. Peter Burke and Roy Porter. Cambridge: Cambridge UP, 1987. 120-35.

_____. *The Body and the French Revolution*. New haven: Yale UP, 1989.

Ozouf, Mona. *La Fête révolutionnaire*. Paris: Gallimard, 1976.

Palmer, R. R. *Twelve who Ruled: The Year of the Terror in the French Revolution*. Princeton: Princeton UP, 1989.

Parker, Noël. "Souveraineté et providence chez Rousseau." *Studies on Voltaire and the Eighteenth Century* 324 (1994): 21-34.

Perkins, Jean A. *The Concept of the Self in the French Enlightenment*. Geneva: Droz, 1969.

Perkins, Merle L. *Jean-Jacques Rousseau on the Individual and Society*. Lexington: UP Kentucky, 1974.

Phelan, Shane. "Intimate Distance: The Dislocation of Nature in Modernity." *The Nature of Things: Language, Politics and the Environment*. Eds. Jane Bennett and William Chaloupka. Minneapolis: U of Minn P, 1993. 44-62.

Proctor, Candice E. *Women, Equality, and the French Revolution*. Westport: Greenwood Press, 1990.

Rétrat, Pierre. "The Evolution of the Citizen From the Ancien Régime to the Revolution." Waldinger 3-15.

Robisco, Nathalie-Barbara. *Jean-Jacques Rousseau et la Révolution Française: une esthéthique de la politique*, 1792-1799. Paris: Champion: 1998.

Roche, Daniel. *La France des Lumières*. Paris: Fayard, 1993.

Rudé, George. *The Crowd in the French Revolution*. Oxford: Clarendon, 1959.

_____. *Robespierre: Portrait of a Revolutionary Democrat*. New York: Viking Press, 1975.

Schama, Simon. *Citizens: A Chronicle of the French Revolution*. New York: Knopf, 1989.

Schmidt, James. "What is Enlightenment? A Question, Its Context, and Some Consequences." *What is Enlightenment?* Ed. James Schmidt. Los Angeles: U California Press, 1996. 1-44.

Schosler, Jorn. "Rousseau et Diderot, critiques de la philosophie égalitaire d'Helvétius." *Revue Romane* 15 (1980): 68-83.

Scott, Joan Wallach. "French Feminists and the Rights of 'Man': Olympe de Gouges's Declarations." *History Workshop* 28 (1989): 1-21.

_____. *Only Paradoxes to Offer: French Feminists and the Rights of Man*. Cambridge, Mass.: Harvard UP, 1996.

Sewell, William H. *A Rhetoric of Bourgeois Revolution: the Abbé Sieyès and "What is the Third Estate?"* Durham: Duke UP, 1994.

Shackleton, Robert. *Montesquieu: A Critical Biography*. Oxford: Oxford UP, 1961.

Smith, Steven B. "Hegel and the French Revolution: An Epitaph for Republicanism." *The French Revolution and the Birth of Modernity*. Ed. Ferenc Fehér. Berkeley: U California P, 1990. 219-39.

Soper, Kate. *What is Nature?* Oxford; Cambridge, Mass: Blackwell, 1995.

Souviron, Marie. "Les Romans de Diderot: une conception philosophique de l'homme." *Europe: Revue Littéraire Mensuelle* 661 (1984): 8-26.

Spaas, Lieve. "*La Nouvelle Héloise*: fiction et révolution." *Studies on Voltaire and the Eighteenth Century* 324 (1994): 49-56.

Spencer, Samia I., ed. *French Women and the Age of Enlightenment.* Bloomington: Indiana UP, 1984.

Starobinski, Jean. *The Emblems of Reason.* Trans. Barbara Bray. Charlottesville: UP Virginia, 1982.

_____. *Jean-Jacques Rousseau, la transparence et l'obstacle.* Paris: Plon, 1957.

Swenson, James. *On Jean-Jacques Rousseau: Considered as one of the First Authors of the Revolution.* Stanford: Stanford UP, 2000.

Tatin-Gourier, Jean-Jacques. *Lire les lumières.* Paris: Dunod, 1996.

Topazio, Virgil W. *D'Holbach's Moral Philosophy: Its Background and Development.* Geneva: Institut et Musée Voltaire, 1956.

Vierhaus, Rudolph. "Progress: Ideas, Skepticism, and Critique: The Heritage of the Enlightenment." Schmidt 330-41.

Viroli, Maurizio. *Jean-Jacques Rousseau and the "Well-ordered Society."* Trans. Derek Hanson. Cambridge: Cambridge UP, 1988.

Wade, Ira. *The Intellectual Origins of the French Enlightenment.* Princeton: Princeton UP, 1971.

Waldinger, Renée, Philip Dawson, and Isser Woloch, eds. *The French Revolution and the Meaning of Citizenship.* Westport: Greenwood Press, 1993.

Weber, Caroline. *Terror and its Discontents: Suspect Words in Revolutionary France.* Minneapolis: U of Minn P, 2003.

Wilson, Arthur M. *Diderot.* New York: Oxford UP, 1972.

Yennah, Robert. "Rousseau et la Révolution: de l'expérience à la pensée dans les *Confessions* et *Du contrat social.*" *Studies on Voltaire and the 18th century* 324 (1994): 35-48.

Index